INQUIRY INTO CRUCIAL AMERICAN PROBLEMS

Series Editor · JACK R. FRAENKEL

Propaganda, Polls, and Public Opinion :

Are the People Manipulated?

MALCOLM G. MITCHELL

Chairman, Social Studies Department
Sequoia High School
Redwood City, California

PRENTICE-HALL, INC.   ENGLEWOOD CLIFFS, N.J.

Titles in this series:

CRIME AND CRIMINALS: What Should We Do About Them?
  Jack R. Fraenkel

PREJUDICE AND DISCRIMINATION: Can We Eliminate Them?
  Fred R. Holmes

THE DRUG SCENE: Help or Hang-up?
  Walter L. Way

POVERTY IN AN AFFLUENT SOCIETY: Personal Problem or National Disgrace?
  David A. Durfee

COUNTRY, CONSCIENCE, AND CONSCRIPTION: Can They Be Reconciled?
  Leo A. Bressler and Marion A. Bressler

VOICES OF DISSENT: Positive Good or Disruptive Evil?
  Frank Kane

CITIES IN CRISIS: Decay or Renewal?
  Rudie W. Tretten

TEEN-AGERS AND SEX: Revolution or Reaction?
  Jack L. Nelson

PROPAGANDA, POLLS, AND PUBLIC OPINION: Are the People Manipulated?
  Malcolm G. Mitchell

ALIENATION: Individual or Social Problem?
  Ronald V. Urick

EDUCATION AND OPPORTUNITY: For What and For Whom?
  Gordon M. Seely

FOREIGN POLICY: Intervention, Involvement, or Isolation?
  Alvin Wolf

THE ENVIRONMENTAL CRISIS: Will We Survive?
  Charles B. Myers

POPULATION AND SURVIVAL: Can We Win the Race?
  Jack L. Nelson

VIOLENCE IN AMERICA: What Is the Alternative?
  Jack Zevin

AMERICAN WOMAN TODAY: Free or Frustrated?
  Elsie M. Gould

© Copyright 1970 by Prentice-Hall, Inc.,
Englewood Cliffs, N.J.
All rights reserved. No part
of this book may be
reproduced in any form
or by any means
without permission
in writing from the publisher.

Printed in the United States of America

ISBN 0-13-730861-2 paper
ISBN 0-13-730879-5 cloth

Prentice-Hall International, Inc.,
London
Prentice-Hall of Australia, Pty. Ltd.,
Sydney
Prentice-Hall of Canada, Ltd.,
Toronto
Prentice-Hall of India Private Ltd.,
New Delhi
Prentice-Hall of Japan, Inc.,
Tokyo

5

PREFACE

The series *INQUIRY INTO CRUCIAL AMERICAN PROB-LEMS* focuses upon a number of important contemporary social and political issues. Each book presents an in-depth study of a particular problem, selected because of its pressing intrusion into the minds and consciences of most Americans today. A major concern has been the desire to make the materials relevant to students. Every title in the series, therefore, has been selected because, in one way or another, it suggests a problem of concern to students today.

A number of divergent viewpoints, from a wide variety of different *kinds* of sources, encourage discussion and reflection and illustrate that the same problem may be viewed from many different vantage points. Of concern throughout is a desire to help students realize that honest men may legitimately differ in their views.

After a short chapter introducing the questions with which the book will deal, Chapter 2 presents a brief historical and contemporary background so that students will have more than just a superficial understanding of the problem under study. In the readings that follow, a conscientious effort has been made to avoid endorsing any one viewpoint as the "right" viewpoint, or to evaluate the arguments of particular individuals. No conclusions are drawn. Instead, a number of questions for discussion and reflection are posed at the end of each reading so that students can come to their own conclusions.

Great care has been taken to insure that the readings included in each book are just that—readable! We have searched particularly for articles that are of high interest, yet from which differing viewpoints may be legitimately inferred. Whenever possible, dialogues involving or descriptions showing actual people responding and reacting to problematic situations are presented. In sum, each book

- presents divergent, conflicting views on the problem under consideration;

- gives as many perspectives and dimensions on the problem as space permits;

- presents articles on a variety of reading levels, in order to appeal to students of many different ability levels;

- presents analytical as well as descriptive statements;

- deals with real people involved in situations of concern to them;

- includes questions which encourage discussion and thought of the various viewpoints expressed;

- includes activities to involve students to consider further the issues embedded in the problem.

CONTENTS

Introduction

    a. All men are mortal.
    b. Tom Smith is a man.
    c. Therefore, Tom Smith is mortal.

The three statements above represent an example of what is known as a *syllogism*. The first statement is called the *major premise*. The second statement is called the *minor premise,* while the third is the *conclusion.* Is the conclusion true?

If you said yes, you are correct! The conclusion is a true statement. Whenever the major and minor premises are true, the conclusion is true. But consider a second example:

    a. All people who live in the Southern part of the United States are bigots.
    b. Bob Thompson lives in the Southern part of the United States.
    c. Therefore, Bob Thompson is a bigot.

Is the conclusion true?

In this instance, it is not. But why not? Isn't this another example of syllogistic reasoning? Well, yes it is. In fact, there is nothing wrong with the steps in reasoning in this example. The syllogism itself is not wrong, but the conclusion is false—because the major premise is false. All people who live in the Southern part of the United States are *not* bigots.

It is important for us to distinguish between *valid reasoning* and *truth.* In trying to influence us, it is a common device for vested interest groups to present an argument in a valid manner, but then to state a conclusion that is false. If people are not careful, it is quite easy to be fooled by what appears to be a perfectly logical argument. Consider the following:

a. Anyone who favors increased welfare payments for the poor is inclined toward socialism.
b. Max Thomas favors increased welfare payments for the poor.
c. Therefore, Max Thomas is inclined toward socialism.

Or this example:

a. Anyone who opposes increased welfare payments for the poor is anti-humanitarian.
b. Philip Green opposes increased welfare payments for the poor.
c. Therefore, Philip Green is anti-humanitarian.

In both of the above cases, the steps themselves taken in reasoning are logical and correct. But again, in both instances, the major premise is false. Because one favors increased welfare payments for the poor does not necessarily mean that he is inclined toward socialism, nor is a person necessarily anti-humanitarian because he opposes such payments.

The art of persuasion is a very old one. People throughout history have, for a variety of reasons, tried to influence other people and have used a variety of techniques to do so. Students of persuasion know that people will react with emotion to certain kinds of "emotionally toned" or "loaded" words. The words "nigger," "wop," "chink," "dago," and "jap" illustrate the point. Different people, of course, react to different words. A clever persuader, therefore, will try to determine which words he can use to help convince others to believe as he does and (hopefully) work in his behalf.

Another persuasive device is to use very general words (sometimes referred to as "glittering generalities") which can have many different meanings to many different people. Who, for example, does not want to be "a responsible citizen," "a patriotic American," or "cool!" Such general words have meanings so vague that almost all of us can endorse them.

There are many other techniques that persuaders can (and have) used. There is the *bandwagon* device, in which an advocate urges us to accept an argument because everyone else is doing so. If we don't go along, he implies, we will be left out (thus the saying "let's jump on the bandwagon"). And not many people want to be "left out." A variation of this trick is the *prestige* approach, in which a famous personality is hired to recommend a product. Hollywood actresses recommend certain kinds of food, and athletes endorse shaving cream. But why should an actress' choice of food or an athlete's opinion of shaving cream be more valid than our own opinion?

Persuasive efforts go on all the time, and they are often very effective. In the United States today, in fact, they can be even more influential because so many more people can be reached through the mass media. Newspapers, magazines, radio, movies, and television messages bombard us daily from all sides. How many of the following slogans seem familiar?

YOU CAN'T DO BETTER THAN SEARS!

WE TRY HARDER

THE GREAT SOCIETY

FORD HAS A BETTER IDEA

IN GOD WE TRUST

ALL THE NEWS THAT'S FIT TO PRINT

PAN AM MAKES THE GOING GREAT

DU PONT—BETTER THINGS FOR BETTER LIVING—

   THROUGH CHEMISTRY

EQUAL JUSTICE UNDER LAW

Now ask yourself: "Where did I first hear those slogans that are familiar?" The chances are it was in one of the mass media mentioned above.

Millions of Americans are influenced by such media. Radio and television commentators express a particular point of view every day in their commentaries on the day's events. No newspaper can print all of the news and accordingly selects only certain items to be included in each day's editions. Documentary films and short subjects often convey emotional or other messages. And who among us has not been at least occasionally irritated by a television commercial?

This is not to imply or suggest that such persuasive efforts are necessarily evil. After all, people can be interested in persuading us to do good things as well as bad. Here, for example, is a message from the United States Committee for Refugees, Inc. Would you consider it to be a message for good or for evil?

Whenever hostilities cease, whenever fighting factions settle their feuds and the war is over, the work first begins . . . the work of resettling refugees in their new country of asylum. Refugees—human beings who fled the ravages of war and political turmoil and religious conflict. Too often, they have nothing to go "home" to. Too often, returning to their former country would mean death or imprisonment. So they choose to stay in their sanctuary. Now, "home" is a mud hut, a shanty covered with broken cartons or flattened oil cans —or maybe just a few square feet of open field. The very young and the very old are ill, dehydrated, undernourished, overwhelmed.

Yet—they have hope. It is only hope for a better future, a better life that keeps them alive. But they need your help! Right now, they need food. Then clothing and shelter. Later, hospitals. Schools. And vocational training. To make them self-sufficient. To plan and work for a better life. To be content. Only then will people everywhere live in peace.

Consider this: It took *fifteen* years to resettle 4,000,000 refugees of the Korean war! How long will it take to resettle today's *18,000,- 000* refugees? From Biafra, Vietnam, the Middle East, Czechoslovakia, Africa, the Western Hemisphere, and numerous unheard of places, these millions of frightened wanderers plead for your help, your compassion. What can *you* do? You can help return these people to the human race! They must be resettled and given every assistance to become productive members of the world society. It takes so little to sustain so many. Won't you do your share? Please send your gift today so that the U. S. Committee for Refugees can bring the desperate plight of these displaced people to the attention of the world.

What is the "message" in this message? Would it move you to act?

The point is that individuals and groups, for one reason or another, try to influence our opinions and, hopefully, our actions. Such efforts to persuade us to think or act in a certain way are often referred to as *propaganda.*

Propaganda is the making of deliberately one-sided statements to a mass audience. It is an act of advocacy in mass communication. Propagandists rely upon every medium or communication—oral, printed, pictorial, plastic, musical, or dramatic.

This book about propaganda will present a variety of readings to help you answer the following questions:

1. How has propaganda as an activity been used in the past?
2. In what forms can propaganda be used?
3. In what ways is propaganda used?

4. Why is propaganda used?
5. What effects can propaganda have upon individuals?
6. How can the effects of propaganda be more clearly understood and handled by us all?

2

The Development of Propaganda

The last chapter gave a definition of propaganda and a few examples of propaganda techniques. This chapter will present a brief survey of some propaganda used in the past, in terms of the definitions of today.

EARLY DEVELOPMENT

Ancient Greece had two practicing propagandists—the philosophers Plato and Aristotle. Plato's *Republic* gives detailed directions on how to keep the people loyal to the state by suggesting what they should and should not be told. Plato advocated censorship to protect the security of the government. He did not feel that the people should be informed about what was really taking place in their country. His ideas about censorship represent a major argument of totalitarian governments for the use of propaganda.

Aristotle's *Rhetoric* calls for the use of more classic methods of propaganda. He wanted to win people by persuasion, by speech. His basic idea was to persuade people to accept the views of the speaker and to reject the ideas of the opponent.

Propaganda was also found in ancient Rome. Parades were staged to honor victorious Roman generals who had returned with riches from conquered lands. These staged processions were intended to impress upon Roman citizens the glory that was Rome. In addition, biased historical episodes were written to arouse patriotism and national pride among Roman citizens. Under the Emperor Augustus, the idea of emperor-worship was developed as a propaganda technique to encourage and retain the loyalties of other nations and tribes under Roman rule. This direct appeal to the religious feelings of subject races was to prove a successful propaganda device, since it appealed to man's basic emotional needs.

CHRISTIAN PROPAGANDA

As the Roman Empire grew, a new kind of propaganda emerged, that of the early Christian missionaries. The apostles went to many lands preaching the gospel to convert anybody who would listen to Christianity. Such preaching proved of considerable significance for both religion and propaganda, and it illustrated another effective method by which people could be persuaded to accept new ideas. Christian missionaries still preach the gospel in many areas of the world today.

In the late Middle Ages and during the Renaissance we find further examples of propaganda. In order to persuade people to join and support the Crusades, which were fought in distant lands, atrocity stories were told of how the Saracens mistreated Christians. This atrocity propaganda during the Crusades was designed to appeal to religious loyalties in order to further war in a remote part of the world. The very word propaganda, in fact, has its origins in the Christian Church. In 1622 the Roman Catholic Church organized the College for the Propagation of the Faith. Its job was to propagandize the teachings of the Church through the use of foreign missionaries. As we have already noted, this practice continues today and is carried on by other religions as well.

In the religious wars of the Seventeenth Century, a new weapon was added to the arsenal of propaganda—the printing press. During this time pamphlets and broadsheets (large sheets of paper like posters) were circulated. Protestants printed leaflets that viciously attacked the Catholic Jesuits, while the Catholics retaliated by calling the Protestants all kinds of names, casting slurs on Muslims, Turks, Pagans, and Jews in the process. The propaganda of both sides claimed divine support for their cause.

THE AMERICAN AND FRENCH REVOLUTIONS

During the Eighteenth Century, the American Colonies carried out a vigorous program of "agitation"—a form of propaganda as old as history—to win military support from France and to gain independence from England. One of the tireless verbal revolutionary agitators was Samuel Adams of Boston. His writing and speaking helped to bring on the split between the Colonies and England that led to the Revolutionary War and American independence.

Another American propagandist was Tom Paine. His celebrated *Common Sense* called for an immediate declaration of independence as the fulfillment of America's moral obligation to the world. His *Crisis* articles, which began with the words, "These are the times that try men's souls," were instrumental in gaining and keeping American support for the Revolutionary War. His pamphlet *Rights of Man,* which Paine hoped would create a revolution in England, was written in support of the French Revolution.

The French Revolution created a new propaganda weapon—the revolutionary song. The Marseillaise (France's national anthem) was deliberately written as propaganda. It was composed in 1792 soon after France had declared war on Austria and when the French Army was faced with an invasion. Its impact on the demoralized French forces seems to have been great. One French general is reported as having said "give me a thousand men and the Marseillaise and I will guarantee victory." (At this point you might remember the words to the Star Spangled Banner by Francis Scott Key and think under what circumstances it was written.)

It was during the Nineteenth Century, however, that the propaganda song came into its own. During that period and after, many national anthems and revolutionary songs were written. Examples include the International (the revolutionary socialists' song for English-speaking countries), the Red Flag (Communist), and the Horst Wessel (Nazi) song.

THE NOVEL AS PROPAGANDA

Novels also were used as propaganda during the 1800's. The most important propaganda novel of the Nineteenth Century was *Uncle Tom's Cabin,* published in 1852. (See page 20 for excerpt.) A still unanswered question concerning this novel revolves around the question of slavery: Did *Uncle Tom's Cabin* do very much towards helping the antislavery movement? Or did it merely reflect an already existing antislavery public opinion in the North? How would you answer this question?

During the American Civil War both the Union and the Confederacy used propaganda to persuade others that their cause was just while their opponent's was doomed to failure. Much of their propaganda was directed at Great Britain. The Confederacy wanted diplomatic recognition and military help from England, whereas the Union strongly opposed these actions. Whether the efforts of either side really affected the political behavior of Great Britain may be open to doubt. But neither was willing to neglect its propaganda effort.

In 1863 a group of workers in Manchester, England, sent President Abraham Lincoln a resolution supporting his Emancipation Proclamation. In so doing, the workers expressed a view contrary to much influential opinion in England. Lincoln replied in an open letter that created some excitement, for in disregard of diplomatic precedent he spoke directly to the people of England:

I have understood well that the duty of self-preservation rests solely with the American people, but I have at the same time been aware that the favor or disfavor of foreign nations might have a material influence in enlarging or prolonging the struggle.

WORLD WAR I

Between the Civil War (1861–65) and World War I (1914–18) most Americans were curious but not really concerned about foreign opinion. Protected by two oceans, weary of the Old World's disputes, and absorbed in the task of building a new nation, America went its own way. When the first World War arrived, however, propagandists began to play a major role.

The first major test of American propaganda came when the United States joined the Allies in fighting Germany in 1917. The American government launched a serious campaign of propaganda abroad. President Woodrow Wilson by an Executive Order created the Committee on Public Information headed by his journalist friend George Creel. The German enemy had corrupted the word propaganda so use of this term was avoided, but propaganda it was, nonetheless.

The Committee on Public Information worked with the Military Intelligence Bureau to send leaflets by gun, balloon, and airplane to German soldiers. Propaganda stories were fed to newspapers in neutral countries. These were often unwittingly transmitted to German newspapers by neutral and even German newspapermen. Books, exhibits, pamphlets, and movies were produced for foreign consumption. Copies of Wilson's speeches and photographs of him were distributed in great numbers. However, the Creel Committee (as it came to be called) was never really popular with Congress, and, as World War I ended, so did the Committee. The idea of the government's being in the propaganda business was too much at that time for the American people to take. Once again the United States turned its back on world opinion.

WORLD WAR II

With the Japanese attack on Pearl Harbor on December 7, 1941, the United States was back in the propaganda business. President Franklin Roosevelt consolidated foreign and domestic propaganda into an Office of War Information (O.W.I.). Its job was to supervise and coordinate all government information functions. The journalist Elmer Davis was appointed the director of O.W.I.

While Generals Eisenhower, MacArthur, and Stillwell encouraged psychological warfare operations, many other military officers thought of war exclusively in terms of men and weapons, not of words. Davis supported those in favor of propaganda when he said that "the war is going to be won primarily by fighting, but we can point to plenty of proof in history that victory of the fighting forces can be made easier by psychological warfare and propaganda." Davis had a realistic view of the role of propaganda during wartime.

Even though Elmer Davis won some converts to his ideas concerning the American propaganda effort, he had only partial success as an advocate and clarifier of American war aims. One O.W.I. official stated later that "while Americans attained considerable skill in the use of propaganda as an instrument of war, they failed completely to develop the arts of persuasion as an instrument of foreign policy."

Despite the failure of O.W.I. to accomplish long-term propaganda goals, it did show its worth in the day-to-day operations in maintaining allied morale, undermining enemy morale, and weakening the enemy's desire to continue fighting.

One example of a simple propaganda scheme took place on January 30, 1943, which was both the tenth anniversary of Hitler's coming to power and President Franklin Roosevelt's birthday. The Nazi Germans were still winning at that point, and Hitler was certain to make the most of the anniversary. When it appeared likely that Hitler would broadcast to the world at 11:00 A.M., it was proposed that the British Air Force bomb Berlin at that exact moment and knock the Nazi radio off the air while the world listened. The idea worked. With perfect timing, British Mosquito bombers hit Berlin a few moments after 11 A.M. *Reichsmarschall* Hermann Goering was substituting for Hitler, who had a sore throat. A few seconds after Goering started to speak, explosions were heard in the background. Shouts and sounds of confusion followed, and then Radio Berlin went off the air. Germany was not invincible, after all. It was probably the only time that German radios broadcast American propaganda.

The O.W.I. helped to shorten the war against Japan by telling the Japanese people that their cause was hopeless. The Japanese government was preparing to discuss surrender without informing the Japanese armies or people. Through radio and massive leaflet drops, the O.W.I. told about the proposed surrender. The Japanese government later admitted that once the people knew about the peace offer, it had no choice but to surrender on our terms. One American official wrote that this "one operation alone probably repaid the entire cost of O.W.I. through the war."

The propaganda effort of O.W.I. did not win the war. It was overwhelming military power that defeated Germany and the atomic bomb that took Japan out of the war. But the American propaganda effort did contribute considerably to the war effort.

THE COLD WAR

When Germany and Japan were defeated and World War II came to an end, many Americans felt that there was now no need for a propaganda effort on behalf of the United States. Many Congressmen felt it was a waste of the taxpayers' money to continue a program of telling America's story to the world. Many Americans also felt that propaganda was not quite respectable. To these critics, it was really nothing more than the big-lie technique developed by the Nazi propaganda mouthpiece, Dr. Josef Goebbels. Nevertheless, William Benton of the *Encyclopaedia Britannica* was given the job of continuing America's propaganda effort, which was not very impressive after the Bureau of the Budget and Congress trimmed the funds available for Benton's program.

One man, however, more than any other, contributed to a growing sentiment in the United States that a strong, permanent propaganda program was a necessity. That man was Josef Stalin. The Soviet Union and the United States confronted one another over many issues during the postwar years. Americans grudgingly faced up to a world in which propaganda efforts by the United States became necessary to explain the basic motives of America to the world.

Congress passed the Smith-Mundt act (1948) "to promote a better understanding of the United States in other countries, and to increase mutual understanding" between Americans and other peoples of the world. The Act provided for "an information service to disseminate abroad information about the United States, its people and politics," and "an educational exchange service to cooperate with other nations in (1) the interchange of persons, knowledge, and skills; (2) the rendering of technical and other services; (3) the interchange of developments in education, the arts, and sciences." Five years later Congress created the United States Information Agency (U.S.I.A.). Why do you suppose it wasn't called the United States Propaganda Agency?

The U.S.I.A. established the Voice of America (V.O.A.), whose job it was to make radio broadcasts to the world in English and other languages describing what life in America was like. With Congress tightening the purse strings, however, these radio broadcasts never did compete in quantity with the number that the Communists broadcast. During a typical year the V.O.A. broadcast a total of 618 hours a week, while Radio Moscow broadcast 997, Radio Peking 997, and Radio Cairo (frequently anti-American) 674 hours. The V.O.A. was later able to up its total programming to 730 hours a week, but the Communists also increased their broadcasts.

THE ROLE OF THE U.S.I.A.

President Dwight Eisenhower and the National Security Council set forth a Statement of Mission for the U.S.I.A. Its purpose was to give a clear picture of the role of the agency:

The purpose of the United States Information Agency shall be to submit evidence to peoples of other nations by means of communication techniques that the objectives and policies of the United States are in harmony with and will advance their legitimate aspirations for freedom, progress, and peace.

A major question arose: How should the United States Information Agency carry out its propaganda effort? Should it concentrate on informing the peoples of the world by means of objective reporting? Or should it attempt to advertise the good and play down the bad about the United States—like soap, perhaps? One critic of the U.S.I.A. has asked "that the

U. S. Information Agency get out of the news business and into the selling business." He calls for "creative programming on the Voice of America designed to reach the largest possible audience with effective messages woven into the broadcast schedule on a day-in and day-out basis. This can bring many millions to our side. The entertainment industry and the advertising industry working together as they do in the United States have proven that they have the know-how to get results."

John Daly, who had been appointed by President Lyndon Johnson to head the Voice of America, resigned over the question of how much truth should be broadcast to the world about the United States. Daly wanted to tell the whole truth about America, but those in charge of America's propaganda effort felt that it was only necessary to broadcast the bare minimum necessary to maintain credibility. The argument over how much "truth" should be broadcast still goes on today.

What Do You Think?

1. Would you argue that propaganda has been important in history? On what grounds?

2. Some people have argued that history, at least as it is usually written, is itself nothing but propaganda. What evidence could you offer to support or refute this idea?

3. Is it necessary that America maintain a continuing propaganda effort in today's world? Why or why not?

4. How much truth should the United States tell about itself to the world—all, some, or none? Explain.

5. What can the United States do to improve its information services to the rest of the world?

3

What Is Propaganda?

In the last chapter you read about the historical development of the use of propaganda in the Western World and the United States. But you still may not be sure just what propaganda is. Can it be recognized? And if so, how? In this chapter we will look at how the propagandist goes about his work to influence people toward a certain end. As you read, try to determine the objective of each example of propaganda.

1. SOME EXAMPLES OF PROPAGANDA

Propaganda messages take all kinds of forms. They are sung, printed, recited, painted, read, and shown to us every day of the year. Here are some examples of the different kinds of propaganda that have been used over the years. Why, and how, are they propagandistic?

Songs

Here are the lyrics to a song written to support General Washington and the American Revolutionary effort. How might you react to this song if you were an American colonist?

WAR AND WASHINGTON

Vain Britons boast no longer with proud indignity,
By land your con–q'ring legions, Your matchless strength at sea.
Since we, your braver sons in–cens'd, Our swords have girded on.
Huzza, huzza, huzza,—For War and Washington!

Ballads

A ballad may also contain a propaganda message. What is the main point of this ballad about Shays' rebellion?

> My name is Shays; in former days
>   In Pelham I did dwell, Sir.
> But now I'm forced to leave the place
>   Because I did rebel, Sir.
>
> Within the State I lived of late,
>   By Satan's foul invention,
> In Pluto's cause against the laws
>   I raised an insurrection.

Public Speeches

An old-fashioned, emotional speech is one of the most frequent methods of propagandizing. Here is the ending of a famous speech. Do parts of it sound familiar?

The gentlemen may cry, Peace, peace! but there is no peace. The war has actually begun! The next gale that sweeps from the north will bring to our ears the clash of resounding arms! Our brethren are already in the field! Why stand we here idle? What is it that the gentlemen wish? What would they have? Is life so dear or peace so sweet as to be purchased at the price of chains and slavery? Forbid it, Almighty God. I know not what course others may take, but as for me, give me liberty or give me death!

Posters

Maybe you have seen the message below (from the Television Information Office) on your school bulletin board or printed in some popular magazine. What is its purpose?

They made sure every TV set would come with a guarantee.

THANKS TO THE FORESIGHT OF THE FOUNDING FATHERS, THE BILL OF RIGHTS PROTECTED BEN FRANKLIN'S FREEDOM OF EXPRESSION. AND IT DOES THE SAME FOR HUNTLEY, BRINKLEY, CRONKITE AND REYNOLDS.

IT'S THE VERY FIRST AMENDMENT. BECAUSE IT PROVIDES ". . . CONGRESS SHALL MAKE NO LAW . . . ABRIDGING THE FREEDOM OF SPEECH, OR OF THE PRESS . . . ," WE'RE STILL GUARANTEED A FREE PRESS.

TELEVISION, BY SHOWING US WHAT'S HAPPENING IN OUR WORLD—GOOD AND BAD—OFTEN AS IT'S HAPPENING, IS AN INTEGRAL PART OF THAT REMARKABLY DIVERSE FREE PRESS—1752 NEWSPAPERS, 1101 MAGAZINES, 6570 RADIO AND TELEVISION STATIONS.

THEIR VOICES—OFTEN IN CONFLICT—BRING US THE FREE FLOW OF INFORMATION AND OPINION THAT IS ONE OF THE MAJOR REASONS WE CAN CALL OURSELVES A FREE SOCIETY.

Leaflets

Have you ever been handed a leaflet as you walked down the street? A leaflet is a direct way to present people with a message. Here is an example of one handed out during a recent school election campaign in California. What is its message?

DO YOU REMEMBER?

The School Auditorium, Wednesday, September 11, 1968

1500 CONCERNED CITIZENS PROTEST FLE
[FAMILY LIFE EDUCATION]

INCUMBENTS UNANIMOUSLY IGNORED EXPRESSED PUBLIC OPINION

If you wish children to be used as guinea-pigs.

If you wish one-third of the District's children to continue reading below grade level.

Then vote the <u>newspaper slate</u> and retain this rubber-stamp Board.

BUT

If you wish to kick FLE right out of the District.

If you wish full value for your tax dollar.

If you wish your schools to Accent Basic Curricula.

If you want a voice in the government of your Elementary School District.

THEN SAY SO APRIL 15

Tracts

A tract is like a leaflet, but it is generally longer and includes much more detail. Here is a headline from one such tract. Does it bother you or not? Why?

WARNING!

YOUR HOME, YOUR FAMILY, YOUR SECURITY, YOUR LIFE IS IN IMMEDIATE DANGER.

If you are a business man, a doctor, a lawyer, a teacher, a politician, a minister or in any place of responsibility or authority . . .

YOU ARE ON THE COMMUNIST'S LIST FOR REMOVAL AND DESTRUCTION

Journals

Many organizations publish magazines or journals to help promote and propagandize their point of view. For example The Freeman (A Journal of Ideas on Liberty) *is published monthly by the Foundation for Economic Education, Inc., a "non-political, nonprofit educational champion of private property, the free market, the profit and loss system, and limited government."*

Here is an excerpt from a recent issue. Does the excerpt suggest the aims of the organization?

The late Lord Keynes and his disciples have heavily bombarded modern man with the theory that he can carelessly consume his way to prosperity. Laws without end have been enacted to implement this false doctrine of consumerism and compulsive spending. Yet, despite that trend, there are those who continue to save and invest in the essential tools of production to which most of us owe our very lives. Call it our saving grace! [1]

Annual Reports

Once every year stockholders receive a report on the financial condition of any corporations in which they hold stock. Usually the corporation puts its best foot forward in telling about the company. Here is an excerpt from the opening Statement of the annual report of Pan American Airways, 1968. Would it create a favorable impression on the minds of Pan Am stockholders?

YOUR COMPANY AT A GLANCE

Pan American World Airways' route system extends over 81,000 miles and provides service between 94 cities in 80 lands. Your Company serves 16 cities in the continental United States, one in Alaska, two in Hawaii, and six locations in United States territories and possessions.

In the past 10 years, since Pan Am pioneered the jet transport as the primary vehicle of the air transport industry, the Company's revenues from air transport have tripled, revenues (passengers per mile) have quadrupled, and net income has increased ten-fold.

Newsletters

Some organizations send out newsletters to members to influence them or to keep them informed. The newsletter below includes a letter written by a local police chief commenting on teen-age drug use in the local community. In what ways is it propagandistic?

LETTER TO TEENS—DRUGS—WHY NOT?

Response to an earlier article on drug abuse and release of the 1968 half year drug arrest statistics dictates additional comment on the drug abuse problem. The State of California Department of Justice reports 15,177 juveniles were arrested for drug violations between January 1968 and June 1968. The 1960 six month total was 728. This represents an unbelievable increase of 14,449 over 1960.

I am directing this article to area teenagers because I feel the answer to the drug problem is largely in their hands. Arrests and adult education provide some controls but not an answer. Today's teenager is going to choose his own adult world. If he does not reverse the trend, the choice will be an unreal, unproductive and (despite the claims of drug users) an unhappy existence.

The marijuana question has been examined by experts from many

[1] Excerpted from Paul L. Poirot, "Our Saving Grace," *The Freeman,* February 1969.

different fields; their positions are as varied as their professions—doctors, lawyers, police, psychologists, ministers, etc. I am opposed to the use of marijuana for many reasons that I believe are valid. However, I am offering only one argument against marijuana in this article. I sincerely believe there is a direct correlation between marijuana use and dangerous drug use . . .

Pamphlets

Pamphlets are cheaper to print than books and can provide a considerable amount of information. Here are a few statements from a pamphlet issued by the Portuguese-American Committee on Foreign Affairs titled "On the Morning of March 15." Do you believe these statements?

The following stories . . . speak for themselves. This is a factual account of some of the tragic events which recently occurred in the morning of a single day in northern Angola. Over 200 Europeans and 300 innocent Africans and mulattos lost their lives on that day. They were tortured, butchered and mutilated with a degree of bestiality that is not condonable on any terms. These few extracts, taken from official sources, tell only a part of the whole ghastly story. Over 50 widely-separate places along a 400-mile front were attacked on the morning of March 15th. These attacks were not just sporadic acts of isolated violence, but part of a carefully prepared plan, instigated and organized outside Angola, and aimed at terrorizing the Portuguese from the country. This plan did not succeed. The Portuguese stood firm despite the hideousness of the initial shock. Many of the terrorists had been carefully primed beforehand with drugs, alcohol and native witchcraft but even so there is a vicious maiming quality and a streak of freakish cruelty about these attacks, which is more reminiscent of dark, barbarian eras than the 20th Century.

* * * * *

The "Primavera" plantation . . . was attacked and all the European personnel were slaughtered. The only survivor was (Mrs.) Reis, the wife of the owner who, after being repeatedly raped, was left for dead. Four white women and five children from the nearby village of Mabinda managed to escape to the woods, where they huddled together in a group while two of their menfolk went to Sao Salvador for help. When they returned they found that the tiny group had been discovered by the terrorists, the women had been violated and hideously mutilated and the children had been hacked to pieces and their remains hung from the branches of trees. Some of the bodies were found with their stomachs cut open and their abdominal cavities stuffed with grass and bits of wood, which had been set alight.

Novels *

It has been said that Uncle Tom's Cabin, *by Harriet Beecher Stowe, helped to bring about the American Civil War. This short excerpt describes how slave children were taken from their mothers and sold. How does this excerpt make you feel about slavery?*

Eliza, a runaway slave, made her desperate retreat across the river just in the dusk of twilight. The gray mist of evening, rising slowly from the river, enveloped her as she disappeared up the bank, and the swollen current and floundering masses of ice presented a hopeless barrier between her and her pursuer. Haley, the pursuer, therefore slowly and discontentedly returned to the little tavern, to ponder further what was to be done. Haley sat him down to meditate on the instability of human hopes and happiness in general.

"What did I want with the little cuss, now," he said to himself, "that I should have got myself treed like a coon, as I am, this yer way?"

He was startled by the loud and dissonant voice of a man who was apparently dismounting at the door. He hurried to the window.

"By the land! if this yer an't the nearest, now, to what I've heard folks call Providence," said Haley. "I do b'lieve that ar's Tom Loker."

Haley hastened out. Standing by the bar, in the corner of the room, was a brawny, muscular man, full six feet in height and broad in proportion. In the head and face every organ and lineament expressive of brutal and unhesitating violence was in a state of the highest possible development. Indeed, could our readers fancy a bull-dog come into man's estate, and walking about in a hat and coat, they would have no unapt idea of the general style and effect of his physique. He was accompanied by a travelling companion, in many respects an exact contrast to himself. The great big man poured out a big tumbler half full of raw spirits, and gulped it down without a word. The little man stood tiptoe, and putting his head first to one side and then to the other, and snuffing considerately in the directions of the various bottles, ordered at last a mint julep, in a thin and quivering voice, and with an air of great circumspection. . . .

"Wall, now, who'd a thought this yer luck 'ad come to me? Why, Loker, how are ye?" said Haley, coming forward, and extending his hand to the big man.

"The devil" was the civil reply. "What brought you here, Haley?"

The mousing man, who bore the name of Marks, instantly stopped his sipping. . . .

---

* Excerpted from Harriet Beecher Stowe, *Uncle Tom's Cabin,* 1851.

"I say, Tom, this yer's the luckiest thing in the world. I'm in a devil of a hobble, and you must help me out."

"Ugh? aw! like enough!" grunted his complacent acquaintance. "A body may be pretty sure of that, when you're glad to see 'em; something to be made off of 'em. What's the blow now?"

"You've got a friend here?" said Haley, looking doubtfully at Marks; "partner, perhaps?"

"Yes, I have. Here, Marks! here's that ar feller that I was in with in Natchez."

"Shall be pleased with his acquaintance," said Marks, thrusting out a long, thin hand. "Mr. Haley, I believe?"

"The same, sir," said Haley. "And now, gentlemen, seeing as we've met so happily, I think I'll stand up to a small matter of a treat in this here parlor. So now, old coon," said he to the man at the bar, "get us hot water, and sugar, and cigars, and plenty of the REAL STUFF, and we'll have a blowout."

Haley began a pathetic recital of his peculiar troubles. Loker shut up his mouth, and listened to him with gruff and surly attention.

"This yer young-un business makes lots of trouble in the slave trade," said Haley, dolefully, [Haley is referring to the fact that slave mothers were often separated from their children. The mothers, naturally, did their best to keep their children, thus causing what Haley calls "lots of trouble in the slave trade."]

"If we could get a breed of gals that didn't care, now, for their young uns," said Marks; "tell ye I think 'twould be 'bout the greatest mod'rn improvement I knows on,"—and Marks patronized his joke by a quiet introductory sniggle.

"Jes so," said Haley; "I never couldn't see into it; young uns is heaps of trouble to 'em; one would think, now, they'd be glad to get clar on 'em; but they arn't. And the more trouble a young un is, and the more good for nothing, as a gen'l thing, the tighter they stocks to 'em."

" 'Wal, Mr. Haley," said Marks, . . . "you say jest what I feel and allers have. Now, I bought a gal once, when I was in the trade,—a tight, likely wench she was, too, and quite considerable smart,—and she had a young un that was mis'able sickly; it had a crooked back, or something or other; and I jest gin't away to a man that thought he'd take his chance raising on't, being it didn't cost nothin';—never thought, yer know, of the gal's takin' on about it,—but, Lord, yer oughter seen how she went on. Why, re'lly she did seem to me to valley the child more 'cause *t'was* sickly and cross, and plagued her; and she warn't making b'lieve, neither, —cried about it, she did, and lopped round, as if she'd lost every friend she had. It re'lly was droll to think on't. Lord, there ain't no end to women's notions."

What Do You Think?

1. Review each of the examples of propaganda that have just been presented. In what ways are they different? Similar? How would you explain these differences and similarities?
2. How would you define propaganda at this point?

2. PROPAGANDA AND RELATED SUBJECTS *

The next reading describes the method, use, and scope of propaganda. As you read this, try to further your own idea of what propaganda is.

First, [propaganda] is not limited in scope to any particular field of life. For the most part we tend to use it in connection with international politics. But not all political propaganda is international and not all propaganda is political. Within the political field propaganda is practised by parties and pressure groups of all kinds, each of them trying to persuade the public to support its cause. And outside politics (in the usual sense of the word) we are all familiar with religious propaganda, as practised . . . by missionaries, and economic propaganda in the form of advertising. To which should be added moral propaganda, a kind of halfway house between political and religious propaganda, since its object is to induce standards of behavior in conformity with both the religion of the propagandist and the political and social society in which he believes.

Secondly, propaganda *induces* the desired behavior; that is to say, the meaning of the word does not include attempts to influence by means of force or compulsion. A slave driver is not a propagandist in any ordinary sense, nor is a member of the secret police who extracts information from his victim by torture. . . .

Thus the central element in propagandist inducements, as opposed to compulsion on the one side and payment, or bribery, on the other, is that they depend on "communication" rather than on concrete penalties or rewards. To affect a donkey's behavior by whipping it, is not propaganda, nor is plying it with carrots. But if its owner shouts at it in a threatening manner, or tries to coax it with winning words or noises, then the word begins to become appropriate.

For—and this is the next point we must note—there is no reason to confine the concept to communications between human beings. It

---

* Excerpted from Lindley Fraser, *Propaganda,* London, Clarendon Press, Oxford, 1957. By permission of the Clarendon Press, Oxford.

extends in the widest sense . . . as the Indian who puts on his war paint before going to battle so as to frighten his enemy or the modern dictator who stages a display of tanks and guns and armoured divisions along the frontier of a weaker neighbor. Each is trying to affect behavior, not by force as such nor by bribes but by direct communication, that is to say, by appeal to the emotions of those to whom the propaganda is addressed.

So the typical propaganda situation is that A by one method or another communicates with B so as to tend to affect B's behavior. Neither A nor B need be a human being, though in what follows we shall be entirely concerned with propaganda from humans to humans. A is the propagandist, while B may be called for lack of a better word the target. (We distinguish here between the target, namely the person or persons to whom the propaganda is directed, and its aim or objective, namely the kind of behavior which the propaganda is designed to bring about.)

Here it may be worthwhile to introduce three further distinctions.

(1) The propagandist, A, may not be aware of what he is doing. He may be an unconscious vehicle of propaganda rather than its deliberate originator. . . .

(2) Propaganda will be either successful or unsuccessful according as the target reacts to it in the way desired by the propagandist. This distinction is of course only relevant to our purposes if the propaganda is intentional. . . .

(3) The objective may be positive or negative according as A's purpose is to effect a change in B's behavior which would not otherwise have taken place or to prevent a change which otherwise would have taken place. One special type of negative propaganda is called counter-propaganda; this name is applied when the anticipated change in B's behavior which A desires to present is itself due to positive propaganda from some other source—as when in war the enemy tries to undermine national morale and the home government launches a campaign to maintain it or when the producer of a well-established branded product increases his advertising appropriation as a result of an assault by a new rival upon his markets. But negative propaganda need not be in the strict sense counter-propaganda since it may be concerned to combat changes in the target's behavior which arise, or threaten to arise, from non-propagandist sources. Thus if changing fashions or theories of health lead to an increase in the number of people who never wear a hat this may lead to a propaganda campaign on the part of hat manufacturers. Or churches may launch a campaign to prevent a drift away from church-going. Neither of these campaigns would naturally be described as 'counter'-propaganda, though they are negative rather than positive, designed to prevent rather than to bring about a change in the behavior of the targets.

Next, let us consider the channels through which the propagandist attempts to reach his target. When the target is an animal it can only be influenced, presumably, through its emotions. But a human target may be presumed also to be capable of reasoning and therefore it is in principle possible to affect his behavior by appealing to his intellect. Indeed, by far the largest part of propaganda, normally so called, makes at least some use of the target's ability to understand. In the case of written or spoken propaganda B's intellect must play its part; in the case of pictorial propaganda it almost certainly does so too, since a poster or advertisement picture must aim at "telling a story" if it has to have a propaganda effect. The only wholly non-intellectual propaganda is that which, like the war whoop of the savage, can be closely paralleled in the animal world.

But if the intellect of the target is essential to almost all propaganda yet it is clearly subordinate in importance to his emotions. We may indeed affect people's behavior by appeals to their intellects alone; but if we do, our activities will not by any standard be described as propagandist. It is not propaganda to teach a child that two plus two is four, though a knowledge of the multiplication table may decisively influence his future behavior in all sorts of areas. It follows that propaganda is at least, to a large extent, emotional in its appeal, whether directly or indirectly.

Yet even here we are dogged by troublesome borderline cases. A missionary, for instance, is clearly a propagandist when he appeals through revivalist meetings to the hitherto sleeping religious fervor of his congregation. But what if by exposition and reasoning he seeks to implant in them the true faith and doctrine of the church? Most of us would hesitate to call this a propagandist activity. And yet the most famous example of religious propaganda was directed precisely to "propagating the faith"; indeed it is to the decision of the Catholic Church in the century following the reformation to set up a special body for this purpose (the Sacra Congregation de Propaganda Fide) that the word propaganda owes its origin. . . .

And more important still the contrast between the rational and the emotional element in propaganda raises, in an acute form, the troublesome question of how propaganda is related to education. . . . We cannot analyse this relationship in terms of the intellect versus the emotions, since that would imply equating education with instruction, or the imparting of knowledge, and most people agree that education means far more than this, including as its main function moulding the pupil's character and implanting in him an attitude to life considered desirable by the educator. Not merely that but the teaching in schools of various non-scientific subjects, and particularly the teaching of history, is almost invariably designed, whether intentionally or unintentionally, to develop certain emotions such as that of patriotism, or belief in a particular social order. Is this not a form of propaganda? In Western countries it would not naturally be so described with reference to education in these countries, i.e., to education for democracy and for love of country. But we in the West find no difficulty in describing the kind of instruction given in and out of school to young people in totalitarian countries—instruction designed to bring them up to be reliable fascists or communists—as propaganda of a peculiarly dangerous and corrupting type. And indeed to the totalitarians what is said and done in schools is an integral part, perhaps the most important single part, of their whole structure of internal propaganda. . . .

On which emotions can propaganda operate, whether directly or indirectly? The answer is, on all of them: simple emotions like fear, complex emotions like pride or the sense of adventure; unworthy emotions like greed, creditable emotions like sympathy or self-respect; self-regarding emotions like ambition, other-regarding emotions like family love. All human emotions and instincts have at one time or another provided propagandists with a means of influencing or trying to influence the behavior of their targets. In some circumstances particular emotions will offer especially promising channels for working on the targets. Thus commercial propaganda tends to make its primary appeal to greed, the desire for comfort, thrift, prestige and ambition. Again, home propaganda in war time relies upon patriotism, family love, hatred and fear of the enemy, confidence in ultimate victory and the sense of courage and even adventure; while propaganda to the enemy may also try to operate on the latter's fear, or it may play on his pessimism and distrust of his leaders or his country's allies. . . . At the moment we need only note, without arguing or illustrating the point, that in such cases the effectiveness of propaganda depends upon the strength of the emotions already existing in the minds of the targets. . . .

What methods of inducement can the propagandist employ in operating on his target? Again we can say, all of them; subject only to the limitations already indicated, namely, that if he uses violence or rewards to achieve his result (as opposed to threats of the former or promises of the latter) he by definition ceases to be a propagandist. It would be tedious, and is unnecessary, to list in detail the methods available to propagandists. The most important of them will form the subject of subsequent discussions. Spoken word, printed work, pictures, patriotic or revolutionary songs, radio, press, pamphlets, leaflets, tracts, "novels with a purpose," satires; public speeches, private conversations and sales talks, rumors; truth, half-truth, quarter-truth, falsehood; one could continue indefinitely the list of weapons in the propagandist's hands, grouping and classifying them in many different ways. Here it will be sufficient to underline one vital point, that concerning truth and falsehood. It cannot be too strongly emphasized that propaganda is as such morally neutral. The propagandist as propagandist will use whatever method he believes to be most likely to achieve the desired effect on the behavior of his target. These methods may be in themselves evil or good, just as the objects which the propagandist hopes to achieve may be evil or good; but neither of these alternatives affects the nature of propaganda as such. . . .

As for the other question, the ends which propaganda is used to serve, there are two things to be said. First, if the ends are good and the propagandist honorable, he will hesitate to use evil means, such as a campaign of systematic misrepresentation, even if by so doing he might increase the prospects of achieving the good ends. If, on the other hand, the ends are evil, the propagandist will presumably have no such scruples. Therefore, secondly, an unscrupulous propagandist will, other things being equal, be more efficient at his propaganda job than a propagandist who allows his skill to be cramped by moral considerations. In a struggle between the two the unscrupulous side is at an advantage, just as it is in the military sphere, when it can make full use of surprise and aggression. If we believe that nevertheless in the propaganda field truth will in the end prevail, that must be regarded as a matter of faith, . . .

What Do You Think?

How would you define propaganda now?

3. POLITICAL SYMBOLS *

Political symbols are objects that represent, or stand for, beliefs and feelings. As such, they can help to arouse emotion. Here is a discussion about political symbols. How do you feel about them? Good or bad? And why?

The relationship between political symbols and political beliefs and feelings can be shown by drawings. For instance, the eagle is a symbol of the United States of America. To loyal Americans, it means strength and courage. It stands for the political beliefs of democracy, freedom, and equality of opportunity. The eagle evokes feelings of patriotism among most Americans.

The bear is a symbol of Russia. The hammer and sickle often shown on the bear's back are symbols of Communism. To most Americans, the bear and the hammer and sickle stand for a threatening enemy who opposes the American way of life. By contrast, the bear and the hammer and sickle would evoke feelings of patriotism among Russians who are loyal to their government. These loyal Russians would view the eagle with fear and distrust, as the symbol of a threatening enemy. . . .

---

* By Howard D. Mehlinger and John J. Patrick, Indiana University.

Political symbols may take many different forms. Flags, medals, buildings, words, posters, uniforms, statues, and music all serve as different kinds of political symbols found in most countries. The American flag and your state flag are political symbols. So is our national anthem. The words "democracy" and "freedom" are also cherished American political symbols. The Washington Monument, the White House, the Lincoln Memorial Statue, and the Liberty Bell are honored symbols of the United States government, as are local court houses, city halls, and Civil War monuments. The uniform of a policeman and the robes of a judge are other examples of symbols.

Political symbols are found in all societies. Why? What is their purpose? What is the function of political symbols in a society?

Following are some comments about the American flag made by ordinary American people. What do these comments tell you about the function of the national flag as a political symbol in our society?

a. Letters to the "Opinion of the People" column of *The Chicago Sun-Times,* June 14, 1967.

   (1) I'm an American and will display the American flag June 14, Flag Day, because I support and am proud of all Amercans serving in the United States Armed Forces.

C. A.

Dekalb, Illinois

   (2) Let every American display Old Glory, the symbol of liberty, righteousness and freedom on Flag Day, June 14. Let us show our pride and gladness by an outward expression of our thoughts. Let us today give thanks for our great American heritage and its attendant favors.

F. C.

Chicago

b. From the *Congressional Record—Appendix*

   (1) Remarks by Father John Myhan. Inserted in the *Congressional Record* by Hon. J. B. Utt of California in the House of Representatives, May 23, 1967.

How often we have seen Old Glory flying proudly in the breeze. How our hearts fill with pride as she is raised slowly to the stirring refrain of the national anthem . . . Wherever she may be, be proud of her, honor her, serve her! For Old Glory represents the greatest nation which has ever inhabited this earth. The stars and stripes represent freedom, and liberty, and justice, and compassion. May she continue to wave. Wave proudly till the end of time.

   (2) Remarks by Judy Covington, eighth-grader of the Dennis R. Smith School in Canton, Ohio. Inserted in the *Congressional*

Record by Hon. Frank J. Lausche of Ohio, in the Senate of the United States, June 8, 1962.

The United States Flag always reminds me of my love and respect for my America . . .

My United States Flag reminds me of the freedoms that Americans enjoy. Many other countries in the world are not so privileged. The Flag means that we as Americans, have the ability to speak, to think, to worship, and to choose our way of life. We may even criticize the government if we so desire.

My flag identifies a democracy where people can work together . . .

What Do You Think?

1. On the basis of the preceding comments about the national flag, what conclusions can you make about the function of political symbols in American society?
2. How does one come to respect certain symbols and dislike others?
3. What symbols can you identify that are important to you? Why are they important?

4. WHY DO AMERICANS GO FOR PROPAGANDA? *

Next, Merriman Smith, a White House reporter, wonders why so many Americans fall for a particular type of propaganda. How would you answer him?

Washington—There is an aspect of the so-called "credibility gap" [see Chapter 6] that has some of the leading government officials puzzled and deeply concerned.

This has to do with an amazing and seemingly increasing number of Americans, to say nothing of untold thousands of persons in friendly countries overseas, who have become so receptive to Communist propaganda concerning Vietnam.

Government professionals, careermen who have no stake in domestic politics or the fortunes of President Johnson are appalled by the number of fellow Americans who if given the choice, believe atrocity from Hanoi or Peking over diametrically opposite versions of Washington, be it from the White House, the Pentagon or the State Department.

---

* From Merriman Smith, of U.P.I., Washington, D. C.

Photographs of burned children and bedraggled Vietnam women with obviously hungry or undernourished babies in their arms from Communist bloc sources are regarded by many Americans as generally representative of a vicious American war effort in Southeast Asia.

Quite naturally the same Communist bloc sources do not service photographs or articles dealing with cases in which the regular North Vietnamese army or members of the Viet Cong have pillaged villages in the south, beheaded village elders or chased family groups into the jungle.

Washington officials do not like to talk about it in public, but they are alarmed that a great many Americans are under the impression that the more brutal aspects of the war in Vietnam are the work of American troops.

A week seldom passes without demonstrators carrying signs in front of the White House reflecting an undiluted propaganda line from Hanoi and Peking.

One has only to travel away from Washington and talk with people at random to discover that a large number of Americans are more receptive to war accounts from Hanoi than they are to presentations by various departments in Washington. And such beliefs are held not only by the more demonstrative members of the far left, but by an increasingly large number of Americans who heretofore have accepted the Vietnamese war largely on face value.

From a recent high-level discussion here came one blunt fact or, in any case, a rather frank opinion from top level officials. This was to the effect that the Communist propaganda apparatus has been at this business a lot longer than the current American government and, as a result, is more effective.

What Do You Think?

Do you think the author is right in believing that Americans fall for Communist propaganda too easily? Explain your reasoning.

5. HOW EFFECTIVE ARE LEAFLETS?

Have you ever considered the fact that printed leaflets are an effective weapon in military warfare? The following article includes some examples. How do they qualify as propaganda?

In the Second World War Germany opened the action on the leaflet front. In the war's early days German pamphlets, like German arms, seemed to have everything going their way. Folders helped take over

Czechoslovakia and defeat France. Leaflets told Frenchmen that the British cremated a living Joan of Arc and Bastilled Napoleon; others showed cartoons of French wives being seduced by English Tommies. Germany bombarded a reeling Russia not only with Stukas and cannon, but with pamphlets proclaiming that Nazi armies included volunteers from all over Europe, specifying such units as the Spanish "Blue" and French "Charlemagne" Divisions.

As the war proceeded, allied forces picked up momentum on the printing as well as the shooting fronts by developing many types of "safe conduct" or "surrender" passes inviting Germans to surrender. Both sides dropped leaflets urging malingering, with headlines like "Better a few weeks ill than all your life dead." The text gave soldiers specific directions for faking amoebic dysentery, eczema and many other pretendable maladies so they could be sent to the rear or sent home, thus depleting the enemy's active fighting force.

The leaflet war was fought on both sides of the world. The Japanese attacked with paper as well as gunpowder projectiles. Hong Kong was "bombed" with leaflets showing an Indian riding an elephant and John Bull riding an Indian. Singapore was hit with fake orders calling for British forces to surrender to the Japanese, by command of General Sir Archibald Wavell.

Slick leaflets showing Yankee soldiers jumping into bed with Australian women were scattered over Anzac units at the Pacific fighting fronts.

American folders functioned as companion weapons with atom bombs to expedite V-J Day. On August 4, 1945, two days before Hiroshima was atom-blasted, the 20th Air Force loosed 720,000 leaflets on a dozen Japanese cities warning that they would be wiped out. Two days after Hiroshima Russia entered the war, and a day later Nagasaki was atomized. In short order leaflets telling of these disasters were rained on many Japanese cities.

When the Japanese Government offered on August 10 to surrender, on condition Emperor Hirohito could retain his throne, everybody in the world knew about it except the Japanese people. The next day Secretary of State James Byrnes replied that the Emperor and the Japanese Government would have to be subject to the command of the occupation forces. There followed silence over Japan while the cabinet debated. The Americans couldn't get the news in by shortwave radio (Japanese jamming) so Washington decided to deliver the word to the Nipponese by printed folder.

The Office of War Information prepared a text and phoned it to Honolulu. OWI Nisei staffers translated it into Japanese on a big placard, which was cut into four quarters and each radiophotoed to Saipan for assembly and printing.

To the Japanese People:

These American planes are not dropping bombs on you today. They are dropping these leaflets instead because the Japanese Government has offered to surrender, and every Japanese has a right to know the terms of the offer and the reply made to it by the United States Government on behalf of itself, the British, the Chinese, and the Russians. Your government now has a chance to end the war immediately.

B-29's dropped three million copies of these political missives over Tokyo and seven other Japanese cities on August 14. On August 15 the war was ended. One of the leaflets had reached Hirohito himself, and the Emperor made this announcement:

I cannot endure the thought of letting my people suffer any longer. A continuation of the war would bring death to tens, perhaps even hundreds of thousands of persons. The whole nation would be reduced to ashes. It is my desire that you, my Minister of State, accede to my wishes and accept the Allied proposal.

Campaign folders as weapons of hard war neither originated nor ended with World War II. More than one hundred different types of pamphlets have been dropped over both North and South Vietnam.

The ancient Chinese, who probably *first* invented gunpowder, also invented paper and may have *first* employed the propaganda leaflet.

According to the *Book of War* written by Wu Sun in the 15th Century, B.C., Chinese armies then included kite flyers who released leaflets over the enemy. Usually they were proclamations offering bribes for desertion. Leaflets were tied to small bundles and attached to kites. A little cord attached to the bundles was then pulled and the leaflets fluttered down. Admiral Thomas Cochrane of the British Navy used kites the same way in the Napoleonic Wars. The Romans and others wrapped leaflets at times about the shafts of arrows and shot them into castles and forts.

Americans first used propaganda leaflets before there was a United States—in 1776, urging the Hessians and the British to desert the redcoat forces.

At the Battle of Bunker Hill, Yankees projectiled rocks behind the British lines with a printed leaflet containing this message:

PROSPECT HILL

    I. Seven dollars a month
    II. Fresh provisions and in plenty
    III. Health
    IV. Freedom, ease, affluence and a good farm

I. Three pence a day
II. Rotten salt pork
III. The Scurvy
IV. Slavery, beggary and want

General Mariano Arista, later president of Mexico, had learned English as a boy in Cincinnati, Ohio. During the Mexican War he tried his hand as a propagandist to capitalize on harsh physical conditions for United States troops. He lured 250 American soldiers to desert General Zachary Taylor and become an artillery battalion in the Mexican Army.

The Arista pamphlet read in part:

Soldiers, I warn you in the name of justice, honor, and your own interest and self respect, to abandon this desperate and unholy cause, and become peaceful Mexican citizens. I guarantee you a half section of land, or 320 acres, to settle on gratis. . . . Lands shall be given to officers, sergeants and corporals according to rank, privates receiving 320 acres as stated.

Abraham Lincoln became a military pamphleteer in the Civil War with a December 3, 1863, proclamation promising amnesty to Confederate deserters. The Franco-Prussian War of 1870 saw the first use of balloons as carriers of propaganda leaflets as well as for the first genuine air mail.

The seriousness with which military commanders view enemy leaflet operations was stressed in World War I. The German high command threatened that captured allied aviators guilty of dropping leaflets would be court-martialed and shot. When they followed this ultimatum by court-martialing two such British aviators, England ordered leaflet drops limited to balloons. Every British combat plane was equipped with a card reading:

"No printed or written matter for distribution is to be carried in this machine. H. A. Lawrence, Lieutenant-General, Chief of the General Staff, British Armies in France."

All kinds of American leaflets, including some depicting hordes of Yankees landing in Europe, were distributed behind German lines. The most effective and well known was the famous "invitation to breakfast."

Write the address of your family upon this card and if you are captured by the Americans, give it to the first officer who questions you. He will make it his business to forward it in order that your family may be reassured concerning your situation.

The message on the reverse card, for delivery to families, read:

Do not worry about me. The war is over for me. I have good food. The American Army gives its prisoners the same food as its own soldiers: Beef, white bread, potatoes, beans, prunes, coffee, butter, tobacco, etc.

The German high command was so dismayed by this propaganda gem that they actually *paid* their soldiers to turn them in. This, of course, directed even more attention to the cards. General Hindenburg then added to the pressure by appealing to German soldiers and civilians to resist the "poisonous leaflets."

The London *Times* wrote that good propaganda "probably saved a year of war . . . thousands of millions in money and probably at least a million lives."

Military warfare has thus for centuries employed the printed piece to penetrate the enemy's mind as it has used hardware weapons to pierce the enemy's body. Having achieved such recognition and application over many centuries as a worthy companion weapon to the bullet in the military arsenal, the printed piece comes with eminent credentials as the foundation stone of the science of political campaigning.

What Do You Think?

1. How much effect do wartime leaflets have on the morale of soldiers?
2. How influenced are people by political leaflets? *Are* people influenced by them? Would you be influenced? Explain how you would be influenced.

6. STATEMENT BY MAO TSE-TUNG *

In his struggle for equality the black man is not overlooked by political parties. Following is an appeal by the Chinese Communists to the black man of America. Do you think it effective?

Some days ago, Martin Luther King, the Afro-American clergyman, was suddenly assassinated by the U. S. imperialists. Martin Luther King was an exponent of non-violence. Nevertheless, the U. S. imperialists did not on that account show any tolerance towards him, but used counter-revolutionary violence and killed him in cold blood. This has taught the broad masses of the black people in the United States a profound lesson. It has touched off a new storm in their struggle against violent repression

---

* Statement by Mao Tse-Tung, Chairman of the Central Committee of the Communist Party of China, in Support of the Afro-American Struggle against Violent Repression," Foreign Languages Press, Peking 1968.

sweeping well over a hundred cities in the United States, a storm such as has never taken place before in the history of that country. It shows that an extremely powerful revolutionary force is latent in the more than twenty million black Americans.

The storm of Afro-American struggle taking place within the United States is a striking manifestation of the comprehensive political and economic crisis now gripping U. S. imperialism. It is dealing a telling blow to U. S. imperialism, which is beset with difficulties at home and abroad.

The Afro-American struggle is not only a struggle waged by the exploited and oppressed black people for freedom and emancipation, it is also a new clarion call to all the exploited and oppressed people of the United States to fight against the barbarous rule of the monopoly capitalist class. It is a tremendous support and inspiration to the struggle of the people throughout the world against U. S. imperialism and to the struggle of the Vietnamese people against U. S. imperialism. On behalf of the Chinese people, I hereby express resolute support for the just struggle of the black people in the United States.

Racial discrimination in the United States is a product of the colonialist and imperialist system. The contradiction between the black masses in the United States and U. S. ruling circles is a class contradiction. Only by overthrowing the reactionary rule of the U. S. monopoly capitalist class and destroying the colonialist and imperialist system can the black people in the United States win complete emancipation. The black masses and the masses of white working people in the United States share common interests and have common objectives to struggle for. Therefore, the Afro-American struggle is winning sympathy and support from increasing numbers of white working people and progressives in the United States. The struggle of the black people in the United States is bound to merge with the American workers' movement, and this will eventually end the criminal rule of the U. S. monopoly capitalist class.

In 1963, in my "Statement Supporting the Afro-Americans in Their Just Struggle Against Racial Discrimination by U. S. Imperialism" I said that "the evil system of colonialism and imperialism arose and throve with the enslavement of Negroes and the trade in Negroes, and it will surely come to its end with the complete emancipation of the black people." I still maintain this view.

At present, the world revolution has entered a great new era. The struggle of the black people in the United States for emancipation is a component part of the general struggle of all the people of the world against U. S. imperialism, a component part of the contemporary world revolution. I call on the workers, peasants and revolutionary intellectuals of every country and all who are willing to fight against U. S. imperialism to take action and extend strong support to the struggle of the black people in the United States! People of the whole world, unite still more closely and launch a sustained and vigorous offensive against our common enemy, U. S. Imperialism, and against its accomplices! It can be said with certainty that the complete collapse of colonialism, imperialism and all systems of exploitation, and the complete emancipation of all the oppressed peoples and nations of the world are not far off.

What Do You Think?

1. What is the author's most telling point? Weakest?
2. What kind of propaganda does this represent?

7. WHERE ARE WE? *

Dr. Martin Luther King, Jr., wrote a book entitled Where Do We Go From Here: Chaos or Community?, *in which he describes the place of the black man in America and speculates about that position in the future. His comments are directed to the white and black community in general. Would you consider his message an appeal?*

On August 6, 1965, the President's Room of the Capitol could scarcely hold the multitude of white and Negro leaders crowding it. President Lyndon Johnson's high spirits were marked as he circulated among the many guests whom he had invited to witness an event he confidently felt to be historic, the signing of the 1965 Voting Rights Act. The legislation was designed to put the ballot effectively into Negro hands in the South after a century of denial by terror and evasion.

The bill that lay on the polished mahogany desk was born in violence in Selma, Alabama, where a stubborn sheriff handling Negroes in the Southern tradition had stumbled against the future. During a nonviolent demonstration for voting rights, the sheriff had directed his men in tear-gassing and beating the marchers to the ground. The nation had seen and heard, and exploded in indignation. In protest, Negroes and whites marched fifty miles through Alabama, and arrived at the state capital of Montgomery in a demonstration fifty thousand strong. President Johnson, describing Selma as a modern Concord, addressed a joint session of Congress before a television audience of millions. He pledged that "We shall overcome," and declared that the national government

---

* Excerpted from Martin Luther King, Jr., *Where Do We Go From Here? Chaos or Community?*, New York, N. Y.: Harper & Row, Inc., 1967. From pp. 1–12. Copyright © 1967 by Martin Luther King, Jr.

must by law insure to every Negro his full rights as a citizen. The Voting Rights Bill of 1965 was the result. In signing the measure, the President announced that "Today is a triumph for freedom as huge as any victory that's ever been won on any battlefield . . . today we strike away the last major shackle of . . . fierce and ancient bonds."

One year later, some of the people who had been brutalized in Selma and who were present at the Capitol ceremonies were leading marchers in the suburbs of Chicago amid a rain of rocks and bottles, among burning automobiles to the thunder of jeering thousands, many of them waving Nazi flags.

A year later, some of the Negro leaders who had been present in Selma and at the Capitol ceremonies no longer held office in their organizations. They had been discarded to symbolize a radical change of tactics.

A year later, the white backlash had become an emotional electoral issue in California, Maryland, and elsewhere. In several Southern states men long regarded as political clowns had become governors or only narrowly missed election, their magic achieved with a witches' brew of bigotry, prejudice, half-truths and whole lies.

During the year, white and Negro civil rights workers had been murdered in several Southern communities. The swift and easy acquittals that followed for the accused had shocked much of the nation but sent a wave of unabashed triumph through Southern segregationist circles. Many of us wept at the funeral services for the dead and for democracy.

During the year, in several Northern and Western cities, most tragically in Watts, young Negroes had exploded in violence. In an irrational burst of rage they had sought to say something, but the flames had blackened both themselves and their oppressors.

A year later, *Ramparts* magazine was asserting, "After more than a decade of the Civil Rights Movement the black American in Harlem, Haynesville, Baltimore and Bogalousa is worse off today than he was ten years ago . . . the Movement's leaders know it and it is the source of their despair . . . The movement is in despair because it has been forced to recognize the Negro revolution as a myth."

Had Negroes fumbled the opportunities described by the President? Was the movement in despair? Why was widespread sympathy with the Negro revolution abruptly submerged in indifference in some quarters or banished by outright hostility in others? Why was there ideological disarray?

A simple explanation holds that Negroes rioted in Watts, the voice of Black Power was heard through the land and the white backlash was born; the public became infuriated and sympathy evaporated. This pat explanation founders, however, on the hard fact that the change in mood had preceded Watts and the Black Power slogan. Moreover, the white backlash had always existed underneath and sometimes on the surface of American life. No, the answers are both more complex and, for the long run, less pessimistic.

With Selma and the Voting Rights Act one phase of development in the civil rights revolution came to an end. A new phase opened, but few observers realized it or were prepared for its implications. For the vast majority of white Americans, the past decade—the first phase—had been a struggle to treat the Negro with a degree of decency, not of equality. White America was ready to demand that the Negro should be spared the lash of brutality and coarse degradation, but it had never been truly committed to helping him out of poverty, exploitation or all forms of discrimination. The outraged white citizen had been sincere when he snatched the whips from the Southern sheriffs and forbade them more cruelties. But when this was to a degree accomplished, the emotions that had momentarily inflamed him melted away. White Americans left the Negro on the ground and in devastating numbers walked off with the aggressor. It appeared that the white segregationist and the ordinary white citizen had more in common with one another than either had with the Negro.

When Negroes looked for the second phase, the realization of equality, they found that many of their white allies had quietly disappeared. The Negroes of America had taken the President, the press and the pulpit at their word when they spoke in broad terms of freedom and justice. But the absence of brutality and unregenerate evil is not the presence of justice. To stay murder is not the same thing as to ordain brotherhood. The word was broken, and the free-running expectations of the Negro crashed into the stone walls of white resistance. The result was havoc. Negroes felt cheated, especially in the North, while many whites felt that the Negroes had gained so much it was virtually impudent and greedy to ask for more so soon.

The paths of Negro-white unity that had been converging crossed at Selma, and like a giant X began to diverge. Up to Selma there had been unity to eliminate barbaric conduct. Beyond it the unity had to be based on the fulfillment of equality, in the absence of agreement the paths began inexorably to move apart.

What Do You Think?

1. Compare Dr. King's idea with those of Mao Tse-tung. In what ways do they differ in tone? Style? Content? In what ways are they similar? How would you explain these differences and similarities?

2.   What impact might each message have upon black people? Which one seems most believable? Explain.

ACTIVITIES FOR INVOLVEMENT

1.   Review the two articles concerning black people to see if you can find any of the following propaganda techniques in them.

a. *Casual oversimplification:* Explaining a complex event by references to only one or two probable causes, when many are responsible.

b. *Rationalization:* Citing reasons or causes in an attempt to justify a certain action, when the reasons or causes cited are not logically related to the action.

c. *Wishful thinking:* Believing a statement to be true because one wants it to be true.

d. *Tabloid thinking:* Oversimplifying a complex set of circumstances. The tabloid thinker prefers quick summaries and has the habit of "putting things in a nutshell."

e. *Emotional terms:* Any words or phrases which arouse a feeling for or against a particular object, event, person, or idea.

f. *Ambiguity:* A word or phrase that can have two or more quite different meanings.

g. *Quotation out of context:* An excerpt taken from a larger statement in a manner that may change or distort the meaning of the original.

h. *Simile and metaphor:* Figures of speech making comparisons of unlike things. A simile uses such words as "like" or "as"; a metaphor makes comparisons indirectly or through implication.

2.   Review all the examples of types of propaganda given in the first reading in this chapter. Hold a class discussion on what steps individuals might take to protect themselves against being unduly influenced by such propaganda efforts.

3.   Keeping in mind several of the forms of propaganda, write some propaganda directed towards teen-agers in the United States. Illustrate your message if possible. Compare your technique and format with that of your classmates. What does the class regard as particularly effective? Why?

4.   Prepare a short research report on how commercial advertising appeals to the teen-age market. Report your findings to the class.

5.   Collect a number of examples of attempts to influence individuals in your community in the last week: e.g., songs, ballads, public speeches (printed in your local paper), posters, leaflets, tracts, journals, newsletters, pamphlets, etc. Classify them—effective, average, or ineffective. Be prepared to defend and explain your classification.

6.   Locate and identify by type (see Activity 1 above and the Introduction to this book) as many pieces of propaganda as you can find in your school. In what ways are their messages propagandistic?

4

Advertising: Buying Soap or a Candidate

In this chapter we will be looking at a more familiar form of propaganda—advertising. Many people do not think of advertising as being propagandistic, but it is one of the oldest forms of propaganda. Every day we are deluged with advertising messages to buy or try this or that. Large advertising firms and public relations organizations spend billions of dollars a year to create a favorable impression on our minds. Today, candidates for political office, including that of the President of the United States, are packaged and peddled like soap. How did it begin?

1. HOW ADVERTISING BEGAN *

Advertising has been around a long time, and old forms of it may still be seen today. What types of advertising do you see in your own community?

In an effort to reconstruct the early origins of advertising, we are going to imagine what may have taken place in the ancient nation of Sumer some 5,000 years ago. We know that Sumer was a nation on an alluvial plain formed by the flooding of the Tigris and Euphrates Rivers, facing the Persian Gulf. It later became known as Babylon and today it is Iraq. We have some samples of Sumerian writing, which are called "pictographs." These writings indicate that by 3,000 B.C. the Sumerians

---

* Excerpted from G. Allen Foster, *Advertising: Ancient Market Place to Television,* New York, N. Y.: Criterion Books, Inc., 1967.

had grouped themselves into cities and villages, which would mean that there was commerce, and thus some primitive forms of advertising. The principal crops of the Sumerians were pomegranates, apples, apricots and barley. Sheep and goats were raised for meat.

Since we know that the marketplace of a Near Eastern village has not changed much in the last 2,000 years, except for the addition of new products, it is reasonable to assume that the public markets of Sumer weren't too much different in 3,000 B.C. from those of today. So let's try to recreate a Sumerian marketplace of ancient times.

The sun is blistering hot. As usual, the marketplace is engulfed in a haze of dust and powdered camel dung. Most of the farmers and shepherds who have come to town that morning have piled their wares in the middle of the narrow street. There are heaps of earthenware, fruit, vegetables, whole sides of lamb and goat, woven fabrics and metalware, all covered with dust and exposed to the blazing sun. The farmers simply squat besides their wares, which are laid out helter-skelter in the dirt, and they haggle over prices with their customers.

But along the walls of the houses facing the street is a row of stalls shaded by rugs hung on poles over the produce. The man in the first stall is selling apples. They are arranged into a neat pyramid instead of being in careless piles on the ground. Also, they have been wiped clean and shiny, and they look delicious. This man is using display advertising to sell his wares. The man in the next booth is selling pomegranates, but he is also a juggler. Keeping five pomegranates in the air at a time, he has attracted a crowd. Dropping the fruit, he proceeds to tell his audience why his pomegranates are the best in the marketplace. He has used an action commercial technique, and his business is brisk.

In the third stall, a competitor of the man in the first, hawks his apples in a raucous Sumerian voice: "Come everybody, buy my fresh apples picked this morning. My fresh apples make the sick well. Eat my apples and stay in good health!" Today, this man would be selling all-purpose vitamin pills.

In the fourth stall, a farmer has several sides of lamb hung on hooks. The meat is obviously fresh, since it is still dripping blood, but it is covered with flies. This man cups his hands around his mouth and shouts, "Commee, commee, commee! Buy my fresh lamb, just butchered this morning. It costs a little more, but it doesn't stink."

But he has a competitor in the next stall who also has lamb. This meat merchant doesn't rely on his voice alone. He dashes out into the crowd, grabs a prospective customer by the robe and almost drags him into the stall. He points to the lamb carcass and exhorts: "Look at that lamb, smell it! Treated with the most expensive, exotic oriental spices. And you won't believe it, cheaper than any other lamb in the market."

He doesn't tell his customer, of course, that the meat was in a stage of decomposition making spices necessary to cover up the smell.

The marketplace of 5,000 years ago may exhibit salesmanship that is primitive by today's standards, but on the dusty, smelly street the basic elements of the most advanced advertising techniques are present. . . . The three basic elements of advertising in any age are *Information, Persuasion,* and *Compulsion.* Variations of these principles were present in the Sumerian marketplace.

The farmers who dumped their apples in the dust of the street were advertising by information only. The presence of the apples clearly stated that they were for sale. "If you want'em, buy 'em." There was no reason given *why* anyone should buy these apples, or any indication that they were better or worse than anyone else's apples.

The man who had polished and arranged his apples in a neat pyramid was offering *information* that he had apples for sale but in addition he had included a bit of *persuasion.* He was attracting attention to his apples, just as they say, "Please listen for a moment," before you begin a persuasive argument.

The man who juggled pomegranates was a strong persuader. He attracted and drew a crowd which admired his agility and thus became more receptive to the purchase of his product.

The first lamb merchant was using a very effective and common technique of *persuasion,* the status symbol. Yes, his lamb cost more than the rest of the meat in the market. But this was a public place, your neighbors were there, and if you bought the more expensive lamb, you must be a "big wheel" or more discriminating in your taste than the average consumer of lamb.

Finally, there was the man with the spiced lamb. He grabbed his prospective customers by their garments to make them come to his stall. This was about as near as he could get to *compulsion.* The Sumerian customer could have yanked his arm away and given the merchant a kick, but this would have created a scene. The best example of *compulsion* in modern advertising is the captive audience, which, in its pure form, is very rare. To an extent, you are a captive audience when you watch television. Unless you have the energy to jump up every few minutes to dial out the commercial, you are forced to listen to it. But a few years ago in Washington, D. C. a bus company installed loudspeakers in its buses which broadcast commercials to commuters. They had to listen— there were no earmuffs efficient enough to keep out the sound. There was no way to avoid the commercials without smashing the loudspeakers. The commuters sued, and the court ordered the loudspeakers taken out.

Since Madison Avenue techniques were already in use (in their most primitive forms) in Sumer so long ago, it would seem logical and tidy to set up a chronological, step-by-step progression of advertising from Sumer to *Clairol,* but it just didn't happen that way. There are really only five periods of definite and sometimes spectacular progress in the history of advertising: from ancient marketplace to Gutenberg's invention of the printing press; from the age of printed "announcements" to the Industrial Revolution of 1830–40; from the early advertising agencies of 1880 to modern advertising *media.*

What Do You Think?

1. How has advertising been used over the years? What kinds of advertising have been most successful?
2. Is advertising necessary? Why or why not? Should advertising always be truthful? Why or why not?

2. THE ADVERTISING MAN *

What is the world of advertising like? In the next reading a senior vice-president of an advertising agency, formerly an account executive, describes some aspects of the advertising business.

My first job was in a promotion department, working from seven-thirty to four P.M. I was seventeen years old. One day my boss called me in and said, "Your problem is that you don't have any selling experience. If you want to get ahead in this business, you'd better put your belly against a counter and sell."

I went out and got a job from six P.M. to midnight, first at the Mc-Alpin Liggett's. The job was for Saturday and Sunday, too. I had Friday night off; Friday nights I took a course at NYU. I learned pretty quickly that I wasn't much smarter than anybody else. But I was willing to work a little harder.

Where I sit now, part of my job is to talk with the messenger boys and the boys in the production department who want to get into client servicing, they want to be account executives. They come up here to me and say, "I'm a salesman, I want to sell." I ask them, "Where does your wife do her shopping, at what super market?" And they don't know. I say to them, "Do you ever hang around a gas station, and find out what

---

* Abridgment of "The Advertising Man: Habitat, Functions and History" from *Madison Avenue, U.S.A.* by Martin Mayer. Copyright © 1958 by Martin Prager Mayer.

people ask for when they drive in?" They look at me as though I'm crazy. . . .

On Madison Avenue or within two or three blocks in either direction are the headquarters of the two largest radio and television networks and the offices of fifty "station reps" who sell advertising time on local stations; the central advertising sales office of almost every major magazine and the editorial offices of such periodicals as *Time* and *Life, Vogue, Look, McCall's* and *Redbook, Esquire* and *Coronet, New Yorker, Mademoiselle,* and many, many others; the main offices of sixty "national reps" who sell white space in a thousand newspapers. Scattered in among them are the advertising agencies themselves, preparing and placing and billing their clients for nearly three billion dollars' worth of advertising a year. Half of American industry's national advertising budget is spent by the agencies of Madison Avenue, and nearly half the remainder by branch offices controlled from New York.

Even before the war this was the home of the advertising business; but Madison Avenue as it appears today is impressively new. New York as a whole has had since the war an incredibly extensive building boom; the new office space added to the city in the past dozen years is greater than the total of all office space, new and old, in any other city in the world. The effects of this construction project are most immediately visible in the Madison Avenue area, where an explosively expanding industry has demanded space for advertising offices, space for communications offices, space for the headquarters staff of manufacturing companies which live by advertising and need a location in the heartland. On Madison Avenue alone more than a dozen new office buildings, each more than twenty stories high, have been built since the war; a block away, Park Avenue below Sixtieth Street has been transformed from a boulevard of old brown apartments and hotels to a nest of green glass, brown glass, blue glass and chrome steel office skyscrapers. Including the new structures on Fifth, on Lexington and in Rockefeller Center, no fewer than forty large office buildings, with little less than twenty million square feet of floor space, have been added to the half of a square mile compendiously covered by the name Madison Avenue.

On the outside, unfortunately, the new buildings are mostly very much alike; on the inside, it is every man for himself. Appearance (the pejorative word is "front") means a great deal in advertising. At the agencies, especially, decor is a means of expression; the agency tries to say something about itself by its use of space, color and design. At Young & Rubicam, for example, the spaces are large, the upholstery material is leather and the color is green—walls, carpets, chairs and couches are green, and the name plaques opposite the elevators on the twelve floors that Y & R occupies announce the agency by means of white letters

against a green leather background. A visitor to the executive floor of
Y & R could be pardoned the feeling that he was in a bank: a long,
spacious deeply carpeted hall broken by a few counter-height partitions
to establish areas for the widely spaced secretaries, doors opening into
obvious (and almost identical) distinction, the monochrome green en-
forcing an impression of solidity. McCann-Erickson . . . uses a collection of correctly restful pastels in the halls and offices of its spanking-new
fourteen-floor New York office, and a visitor to the executive floor of
McCann could be pardoned the feeling that he had stumbled into a movie
set: a vast center area almost as wide as a city street with secretarial
desks of luxurious modern design, elaborately simple chairs and couches
in black, red and yellow scattered for the ease of important people who
have personal appointments but will have to wait. . . .

Advertising men, in fact, rarely get much time away from their jobs.
They work in a windy atmosphere of shifting preferences, where crisis
is a normal state of affairs and (as an advertising manager puts it)
"Somebody is always hitting the panic button." No job is ever really
completed except when catastrophe sweeps all the work away, and each
individual is under constant pressure to produce more ideas, new ideas,
better ideas. Every night the brief cases and attache cases go home stuffed
with work, because the advertising man is paid for his production, not
his time, and the industry expects every man to do his duty whether he
is in the office or eating lunch, on the commuter train or in the bosom
of his family.

This is where advertising in real life departs most radically from
the public image of the trade; the best people in advertising work terribly
hard. There is literally no limit to the amount of information—about
markets and products, people and their habits, the past and the future—
which ought to be in the advertising man's head, ready to be pulled out
for examination when questions are asked. The learning process is con-
tinuous, and the material to be digested is often difficult; and, once the
advertising man has learned all there is to learn, he cannot sit back and
admire his accomplishment. He is supposed to *do* something which will
somehow change the situation. He gets paid for doing, not for learning. . . .

Advertising is a [three-part] business, composed of clients (the companies which make the branded products and pay to advertise them),
agencies (which prepare and place the ads), and media (the newspapers,
magazines, broadcasting stations—each an individual *medium* for advertising—which carry the message to the public). In each of its parts and
as a whole, advertising is a salesman's business; all advertising work is
essentially selling work. Within the client corporations, the advertising
manager's primary job is to sell a budget to the sales manager or to some
personage even more august; the agency must sell the value of its service

to advertisers; the media must sell to both agencies and advertisers their potency and efficiency as message carriers. And the industry in its entirety exists solely for the purpose of selling goods and services to the consuming public. . . .

Only the very brave or the very ignorant (preferably both) can say exactly what it is that advertising does in the market place. The relative efficiency of advertising as a selling tool is arguable on the national scene and within specific industries. But advertising to the millions is unquestionably more efficient—less expensive per dollar of sales produced—than the old methods which saw individual salesmen working over individual customers. There can be no return to personal selling; capitalism is finally committed to the intensive use of advertising.

This commitment, however, has carried with it a certain amount of embarrassment for everyone concerned. Selling by means of a personal sales force is visibly profitable or unprofitable: each salesman sells so many units, and the profit on those units either does or does not cover the salesman's salary, commissions and expenses. In the usual course of events, however, it is impossible to discover how many sales have been made by advertising, or whether more or less profit would have come onto the books if the advertising budget had been greater or smaller. Most advertisers probably *do* make money by their advertising, but the standard business-school thesis that companies advertise to increase their profits represents the *excuse* at least as often as it represents the *reason* for advertising.

A quick glance at the community of advertisers will show the diversity of proximate causes for advertising:

Here is a man with a patent mousetrap, who is selling it by mail order: he advertises today to make cash next Thursday, and counts his coupon returns. (The Literary Guild's profits on new one-year memberships exceed its advertising costs.)

There is a man with a painkiller which will relieve pain more quickly in people susceptible to suggestion: he advertises to help his product work on its consumers. (Miles Laboratories spend some $9 million to advertise Alka-Seltzer. . . .)

In the temporary office upstairs is a member of the executive committee of a billion-dollar corporation which sells only to other manufacturers, never to the public: he advertises to make points before Congressional committees and the anti-trust division, sometimes to convince the public that his organization is not a mere commercial enterprise but a beneficent institution. (Du Pont, by advertising, has changed itself from "Merchants of Death" to "Better Things for Better Living, Through Chemistry.") . . .

Most of all, however, companies advertise because advertising satisfies that overwhelming need for security which afflicts business *organiza-*

tions in a highly developed capitalist economy. Brand names have a social value, because they assert the manufacturer's responsibility for the goods he sells, but there is no business need for them. Many manufacturers do splendidly, selling unbranded products to food and variety chains, department stores, and even local liquor stores for these retailers to market under their own labels.

The major reason why many companies brand their products is the desire to free themselves from dependence on their jobbers and retail dealers, to build a "franchise" with the public at large. While no manufacturer ever escapes entirely from the personal element—even those who do no more than write letters to their dealers gain or lose sales by their phrasing of the letters—a business built around a brand name does not have to worry about its future when the popular sales manager, or the president with a genius for distribution, passes on to his final reward. Organizations, like individuals, have an instinct for self-preservation, though the instinct had developed in different degrees in different companies. The drive toward "committee management," toward the development of what William H. Whyte has called "the organization man," stems from this need for assurance that the business will survive the death or retirement of the men who have been running it. And the insistence on ever-larger advertising budgets grows at least in part from this irrational need rather than from a reasoned appreciation of the profits to be made by advertising. . . .

Most people who speak of advertising as a game think of the game as something simple, like spin-the-bottle; actually, the game of advertising is a classic game, as complicated as chess. What the advertising man loves in his work is the constant testing of his efforts, the mysteriously changing numbers that measure, or seem to measure, his success or failure. The client's marketing problem is developed and analyzed, the advertisements prepared and presented. A few weeks later the Starch figures come in, reporting how many people saw the ad and read it and noted the product it advertised, and how the ad stacked up in these respects against other advertisements for similar products. Later, a client emissary delivers the thick reports from Gallup & Robinson, verbatim transcripts of what people who noticed the ad or the commercial had to say about it, what they thought the sales arguments were, and how important and believable the arguments seemed to them. Then the advertising man examines the new Nielsen index for his product, and sees how sales figures moved while the ads were running, the degree to which the product he advertised increased its share of market or loss ground to its competitors. Finally, the value of the effort as a whole is measured by the client with the one simple number that emerges from all the complexities: the size of next year's advertising appropriation.

The advertising man in the typical case needs the challenge and the thrill of the numbers game as much as he needs his salary. Advertising is selling, and the great satisfaction of selling is closing the sale. The advertising man never can close a sale; in fact, he can never be certain that it was his effort which made the sale possible. Worst of all, he works in black anonymity. Everybody in America may know his ad, but not one citizen in a thousand will know so much as the name of the agency which prepared the ad, and within the agency only a handful of people will know that this individual advertising man had anything to do with the ad. He is a cog in a little wheel that runs by faith inside a big wheel that runs by the grace of God; he puts his shoulder to the job, and watches eagerly for measurements of how fast the wheels are spinning.

What Do You Think?

1. Would you consider this a biased or unbiased version of what advertising and advertising people are like? Explain.
2. Can you contradict or argue against the views presented in this reading in any way? Explain.
3. What additional information would you want to obtain before deciding on an advertising career?
4. Is advertising a form of propaganda? Why or why not?

3. ADVERTISING'S PERMISSIBLE LIE *

Here is another view of advertising. Do you agree with it?

The Reader's Digest Association, which bought Funk & Wagnalls at the end of 1965, recently withdrew from publication Samm Sinclair Baker's book about the advertising business, *The Permissible Lie,* a few days before it was to have been distributed to book stores, although 5,500 copies already had been printed. Subsequently, the World Publishing Company picked up the book, altered the imprimatur to bear a *World* imprint instead of F & W's, and has since gone to press with another 5,000 copies because of the enormous publicity attendant upon the *Digest's* amazing action. *The New York Times* said of the event that it was the "first instance of such censorship in book publishing history," and this may well be the case since nothing even approximating such an action

---

* Excerpted from Richard L. Tobin, "Advertising's Permissible Lie," *Saturday Review,* August 10, 1968. Copyright 1968 Saturday Review, Inc.

comes to memory. The book was withdrawn because it had been found contrary to the best interests of *Reader's Digest,* which once took no advertising at all.

Actually, the action seemed hardly justified by the contents of the book, which is relatively mild and repeats many of the half-truths known to anyone who has ever worked on Madison Avenue. For example, to prove Rapid Shave's super-moisturizing power, one TV ad put the shaving cream on what appeared to be rough sandpaper. Thereupon the sandpaper was shaved quickly and clean, implying that Colgate-Palmolive had a product that would soak any beard rapidly and thoroughly enough to facilitate shaving. The trouble was that the sandpaper used on TV was, according to Samm Baker, really a sheet of Plexiglas to which sand had been applied because real sandpaper had to be soaked in Rapid Shave for more than an hour before its "whiskers" were off in a stroke.

Another item involved test trickery. Lavoris mouthwash was, said the TV ads, best by test against mouth odor. However, Baker states, by no means all mouthwashes were compared, only sixty people were tested, no drink and food were taken during the three-hour test period, and the testing method of direct mouth-to-nose technique was highly unscientific. Again, Bayer Aspirin, Excedrin, Bufferin, and Anacin each claimed to be stronger than the other three, for a variety of reasons. The truth of the matter, according to the Federal Trade Commission, is, in Baker's words, that "each of the various analgesic products is effective to essentially the same degree as all other products supplying an equivalent quantity of an analgesic ingredient or combination of ingredients."

Madison Avenue appears to have a fixation with the word "new" and/or "improved." Scarcely an hour goes by on TV that the viewer is not inundated with claims by products that are "new" and "improved" and sometimes both. Baker quotes a housewife overwhelmed with such pleas for purchase: "It makes me wonder just how horrible the stuff was that they *used* to try to sell me." This approach and psychology have always baffled us anyway. Just as we become used to a rather pleasant toothpaste said to be efficacious in reducing cavities we are shown a housewife or her mother or husband throwing the old product into the wastebasket half used and we are then enjoined to replace it with a new mint-flavored dentifrice. If knocking today the product you sold yesterday in supposed good faith to a panting public is sound salesmanship, then we don't know anything about a business we've been in and around for more than forty years.

As to cigarette advertising on TV, the claims and counterclaims are so patently absurd, the testimonials so ludicrous and, in many ways, so dangerous, particularly to the young and impressionable, that we read with great interest the other day the Federal Trade Commission's proposed edict to throw all cigarette advertising off the air. If you want to see really trenchant TV advertising involving cigarettes, don't miss the American Cancer Society's latest sequences "like father like son," for our money one of the most effective campaigns ever used anywhere.

To get back to the book itself, Baker criticizes Madison Avenue not only for condoning but encouraging half-truths and exaggerations. He adds: "The overwhelming aim of advertising is to make a profit; to serve the public becomes a secondary consideration. A lie that helps build profits is considered a permissible lie." However, Hobart Lewis, president and executive editor of *Reader's Digest* stopped publication of the book by Funk & Wagnalls on grounds that "Advertising is good for business and business is good for the country. *Reader's Digest* has a point of view and, it seems to me, has a right to its point of view. Funk & Wagnalls is not an independent publishing house but our subsidiary."

We have never quite understood why advertising seems to think it has to be irritating, vulgar, and extravagant; nor have we ever found anyone who was persuaded by a TV fantasy, usually taking place in someone's kitchen, in which one floor-sink cleaning compound out-dazzles another one with a single stroke of mop or sponge. Similarly no one in the soap business can have the slightest sense of humor if he has anything whatever to do with the perfect cataract of claims of one detergent giving the housewife whiter wash. Someone's got to be wrong; they can't all be whiter. And we must say we applaud Baker's quote from *Printers' Ink:* "In a single half hour of browsing through magazines, I found more than a dozen ads claiming that their products were smoother; longer-lasting; cheaper; better; washed whiter; stayed fresh longer. . . . Are we really suckers that we swallow these pointless hooks? I doubt it—and I think the public is being cheated by the manufacturers if there is nothing more to be said about their products or the manufacturers are being taken by their agencies if this is the best copy they can turn out." It would be difficult to say it better than that.

What Do You Think?

1.   Compare this view of the advertising business with that presented in Reading 2. Which would you endorse? Explain your choice.

2.   Can you think of any other examples similar to those suggested in this reading?

4. THE BUTTON CRAZE *

In recent years buttons of various types and sizes, with widely vary-ing messages, have appeared throughout the world. Just what is their appeal?

"Buttons are the newest phenomena in the advertising and public relations fields," writes *The New York Times* in a December, 1966, fea-ture story.

Perhaps so, but in the political field they are probably as old as the caveman's club.

Apparently this political outcropping, and some of the instincts that go with it, are becoming a year-around manifestation in the United States. Avis Rent-A-Car put out eighteen million "We Try Harder" buttons in twenty-one different languages, making free advertising foot-soldiers of millions of nonemployees. Continental Can put out a "We Like It Here" button observing its fifteenth anniversary in Milwaukee. The gimmick was snapped up by Wisconsin's governor for a big state promotion cam-paign.

General Electric put out 850,000 buttons in a public service pro-gram to decrease dropouts. Different slogans emphasized that everybody can be a genius in some way.

Psychologist Harold Greenwald opines, as quoted by Leroy F. Aarons in the Los Angeles *Times,* "Shy people wear them to get attention and as a way of communication without speech. The button-wearing boom may be partially due to people's unconscious need to establish some identity in an over-organized, mechanical society which tends to beat down the individual personality."

One entrepreneur of political or nonpolitical buttons—and most of them at least have political overtones—shipped 100,000 a month all over the country to book stores, boutiques, sexual freedom groups, anti-Vietnamiks, reform societies, peace promoters, utopians, and anybody who will buy them.

Some of the "best sellers" of the mid-sixties include:
Let's Legalize Pot
Make Love, Not War
God is Alive and Well in Mexico City
End Poverty—Give Me $10.00

---

* Excerpted from Herbert M. Baus and William B. Ross, *Politics Battle Plan,* New York, N. Y.: The Macmillan Company, 1968.

Repeal Inhibition
Support Mental Health or I'll Kill You
Ban the Bra
Kill for Peace
Down with Sex
The World is Flat

There's a button for every point of view. There is "End Poverty, Give me $10.00" versus "I Fight Poverty—I Work." There is "War Is Good Business—Invest Your Son" versus "Bomb Hanoi." There is "Support Your Local Police" versus "Your Local Police Are Armed and Dangerous."

Many are quite nasty, but the more outrageous the copy, the greater the gut reaction inspired in some of the contentious clientele. However, one factory turned down copy containing a dirty word, and another rejected "Ronald Reagan for Fuehrer" because it featured a swastika and the Jewish employees of the supplier would have nothing to do with handling it.

The big guns of political campaign promotion are the massive TV campaigns, the big press conferences, and press-radio TV news, the lavish billboard displays.

But millions of dollars are also spent on the flotsam and jetsam— the trinkets and gadgets and gimmicks which campaigns and headquarters buy—buttons and many a thing more—to give the volunteers to wear, hand out, or use for decorations.

The Republican National Committee, for example, lists several dozen companies all over the country which manufacture, sell, and ship such political tidbits as bumper strips, window stickers, buttons, pens, pencils, emery boards, sewing kits, thimbles, posters, ash trays, caps, visors, balloons, identification cards, flags, banners, bunting, auto reflectors, auto signs, badges, balls, piggy banks, bookmarks, bottle caps, milk bottle collars, combs, cookie cutters, decals, model animals, model cars, fans, feathers, grip discs, handkerchiefs, hats, head bands, jewelry, litter bags, napkins, neckties, playing cards, pot holders, sound equipment, stamps, stationery, and book matches.

There's something for everybody. If headquarters doesn't order first, the salesmen will be around even as sellers of life insurance or Fuller brushes never miss a home. Just get the slogan on it and spell the candidate's name right, please. And allow three weeks for shipping.

As a Republican campaign manual said, "Contributions can be taken for the items. Numbers of groups all over the country raise large sums of money this way and help substantially in filling the campaign coffers. When you select items do not get just the things you like. There are a variety of tastes among the more than 190 million Americans."

How long will it take them to get Blue Chip or S & H Green Stamps into the political paraphernalia parade? No longer than the next election, in all probability.

But lest anybody think there's anything new about it, in 1879 N. Eames & Company of 46 West Broadway, New York City, advertised in *Harper's Weekly* a line of "banners, caps, capes, torches, shirts, belts, campaign tenor drums, transparencies, flags, streamers, bunting. Eames' 'official' campaign badge, portraits of candidates in six oil colors, Presidential grand march song book, fireworks, colored tableaux, lights for meetings at night, embracing more articles than all other dealers combined."

What Do You Think?

1. Do political buttons have more impact on the person wearing them or the person seeing a button on someone else?
2. Why do people wear buttons? Do you?
3. Do you consider buttons a form of advertising? Of propaganda? Explain.

5. OUTDOOR ADVERTISING *

Next, we gain some insight into the power of billboards.

As long ago as ancient Pompeii, before Vesuvius, writes *Life* magazine:

Professional sign-painters plastered walls all over the city with pleas to vote for this or that politician before each year's election. Ordinary people, perhaps inspired by this, felt impelled to scratch down anything that came into their heads on any handy wall. These scratched writings are called *graffiti*. Such remarks as "Samius to Cornelius; Go hang yourself" and "Romula tarried here with Staphylus" are still visible on the walls. Children practiced their alphabets up as high as they could reach, lovers wrote their girl friends' names, and one exasperated Pompeiian scrawled in at least three different places that "It is a wonder, oh wall, that thou hast not yet crumbled under the weight of so much written nonsense."

The same thing is going on in today's space age; there's just a different crowd doing it.

---

* Excerpted from Herbert M. Baus and William B. Ross, *Political Battle Plan*, New York, N. Y.: The Macmillan Company, 1968.

Outdoor advertising does not an election win—but it helps above all in keeping up the spirit of the campaign troops.

As with military air cover, the presence of strong outdoor advertising support, usually set up one to two months in advance of election, depending upon the campaign's affluence, comforts the campaign supporters with the feeling that they are not alone, there is something doing, strength behind the campaign is there for all to see.

While comforting the home team, the strength of an outdoor showing puts pressure on the opposition. It upsets them to see their adversaries show more strength than they display, or have harder-hitting paper on the boards.

Not the least important morale factor is what a good billboard showing does for the candidate himself.

When all seems awry—the volunteers are waspish, the finance committee is bogging down, the bills are mounting in size and number, the commentators are becoming shrill, the newspapers are tightening up on space, the cartoons are becoming brutal, the coffee hours are piling up in number but going down in average attendance, the schedule is becoming too busy and boring—then the billboards go up.

For the candidate it is one of the beautiful days of the campaign. It makes travel about the area much more tolerable, even inspiring.

This is not to speak about the candidate's wife and children. "Oh, Daddy, that's *such* a handsome picture." "Henry, dear, your billboard makes all the other candidates look second rate." And so it goes. Everybody is happy for a day.

Overshowing is to be avoided. Too much billboard saturation can make a campaign seem too rich, cause a feeling of distaste, stir up a reverse psychology.

Smaller billboards, usually approximately one-fourth the size of standard "twenty-four" sheets, pack plenty of punch, cost less, and by seeming to be a poor man's outdoor advertising, tend less to stir up the "that fellow's too rich" syndrome.

The location of outdoor advertising posters is always a dependable source of headaches for the campaign manager. There will be an eager beaver (a bevy of them usually) in every campaign who wants to check the signs, and he may (or they may) be relied upon to miss from 5 to 20 per cent of the showing because amateurs can *never* read and understand an outdoor assignment list and find some shifting of locations because the outdoor advertising company loses locations—old buildings are torn down, new buildings are put up, the owner breaks the lease or any of a dozen more reasons.

Outdoor will usually be the first medium contracted for by campaign management, because while newspaper space usually is available in unlimited quantity until the physical deadline on the very eve of election, the radio and TV spots are available in healthy quantity until a late hour, outdoor locations are strictly limited. It seems there are never enough to go around.

The secret of outdoor advertising success is to buy early in ample supply. The billboard market is so tight in some places that even a far-sighted campaign manager with ample funds is restricted and may get only a fraction of his needs. But if he waits he will get nothing.

The campaign manager in a billboard squeeze can go to friendly businessmen who have large showings and induce them to release boards for his candidate. It can be harder than raising money. Greater love hath no advertiser than to let go of part of his precious outdoor showing in behalf of the candidate of his choice.

The highest and best use of outdoor advertising was illustrated in the first campaign for office of Sheriff Peter Pitchess of Los Angeles County. Pitchess had the warmest regards of the insiders aware of his potential, but to the general public at that time he was a political unknown with an unusual name, hard to spell and pronounce. A heavy billboard showing, hammering home the PITCHESS name connected with a strong and manly photograph, was the trump card of the campaign. It elected the new sheriff over three contenders with one of the biggest vote pluralities ever registered in the giant county.

What Do You Think?

1. Are billboards necessary? Why or why not?
2. To what extent are people influenced by outdoor advertising?
3. Many people have argued that billboards do more harm than good in that they disfigure much of the natural countryside. How would you respond to this statement?

6. THE SMOKE-FILLED AD AGENCIES

Next, we get a look at a special kind of advertising agency—one specializing in political management. Are such specialized firms desirable or not?

A Positive View *

The words on the office door say simply: Spencer-Roberts, Inc.—Advertising. There are no campaign posters, no political hangers-on lounging

---

* Excerpted from Peter Bart, "The Smoke-Filled Ad Agencies," *The New York Times,* July 10, 1966. © 1966 by The New York Times Company. Reprinted by permission. As excerpted by *Current.*

in the corridors. Yet within this drably furnished suite of offices, a team of professional political managers . . . [is] busily laying plans . . . for the governorship campaign of Ronald Reagan, . . .

Stuart Spencer and William Roberts are neither party functionaries nor members of Mr. Reagan's personal staff. They run the Reagan campaign as they have run many others in the past, for candidates ranging from Governor Rockefeller to John Rousselot, who is now the public relations director for the John Birch Society. . . .

Spencer-Roberts, Inc., its methods and its political philosophy, has become a topic of ever-mounting discussion and controversy in political circles. At least one respected national Republican figure believes that Spencer-Roberts has become the prototype for similar political management firms emerging around the nation. . . .

This new prominence has had its unpleasant side effects, however. The decision of Spencer-Roberts to handle the Reagan primary campaign . . . caused deep resentment in the liberal-to-moderate strata of the party.

Friends of Sen. Thomas H. Kuchel, whose campaign Spencer-Roberts piloted in 1962, say the Senator was deeply disturbed by this "switch" to the conservative wing of the party and that, as one prominent Kuchel man puts it: "This will ruin them with the moderates." Mr. Spencer and Mr. Roberts have expressed surprise to associates over this bitter reaction. "They feel they're political pros who are above this sort of ideological bickering," says one Republican official.

Ironically, Spencer-Roberts was not the only political management firm to switch ideological sides this year. Another California firm, Baus and Ross, Inc., which handled the Goldwater primary campaign in California in 1964 against Governor Rockefeller, has gone over to the Democratic side. . . .

"There's nothing wrong with fighting to save California from being run by a movie actor," says William B. Ross, a partner in the firm. Hence, only two years after working for Mr. Goldwater, Baus and Ross says it will be pinning the "Goldwater philosophy" on Mr. Reagan. And Spencer-Roberts, which fought the Goldwater wing two years ago on behalf of Mr. Rockefeller, is now championing its cause.

While Baus and Ross has specialized in bond issues and state propositions—the company ran the successful campaign two years ago to ban pay television in California—Spencer-Roberts has cast its lot entirely with political candidates, ranging from the local to the statewide levels.

Former "clients" think highly of their work. "They're good technicians," said Mr. Rousselot, who hired Spencer-Roberts to work on his Congressional campaign in 1960. "They know practically every Republican worker in the state and they know who can produce and who cannot. If they had handled Goldwater in 1964, I thing he would have done even better." Mr. Rousselot tried to hire Spencer-Roberts again in 1962 but by then the firm was working on Senator Kuchel's Senatorial campaign.

Former clients suggest that the firm's greatest strength is in committee organization, mobilization of campaign workers and handling of mass mailings. As the firm has prospered, it has been investing funds in computer techniques for politics and recently set up a new subsidiary, Datamatics, Inc., to specialize in this approach. One Datamatic job has been to build an elaborate mailing list of 50,000 Republican activists in Southern California. These names are fed into a computer in a way that enables the firm to form mailing lists broken down by occupation, residence and shade of political opinion. . . .

Spencer-Roberts was credited with a major role in Mr. Reagan's expertly staged announcement of his candidacy. . . . The announcement involved a series of carefully planned events, a massive new conference, a reception for 6,000 supporters, a dinner with community leaders and finally a polished 30-minute television special beamed throughout the state.

While working closely with Mr. Reagan, Spencer-Roberts insists that it has not devised his speeches or sought to influence his ideology. Spencer-Roberts is widely assumed to have played a major role in helping to "moderate" Mr. Reagan's political image, but the firm insists that Mr. Reagan was a "moderate" to begin with.

A Negative View *

Advertising firms have a legitimate part to play in election campaigns; but the cool professionalism of their operations in California politics is chilling. . . . If their work were limited to technical services—preparing layouts, scheduling advertisements, arranging television appearances and the like—it would make little difference. . . .

But, while they may not be quite the "kingmakers" they are reputed to be, they are clearly more than mechanics. When a company that took fees from the Goldwater people two years ago now plans to pin the "Goldwater philosophy" on Reagan, it is coldly mapping strategy. When a company that a few years ago ran the campaign of John Rousselot, a Birch Republican, now works to present Mr. Reagan as a moderate Republican, it is in the business of projecting images for profit—any image that will pay.

Admittedly, campaign "corn" goes back to the early days of the Republic and so does the creating of "personalities." When William Henry Harrison's strategists promoted him as a log-cabin-and-cider-barrel

---

* Excerpted from an editorial in *The New York Times,* July 19, 1966. © 1966 by The New York Times Company. Reprinted by permission.

candidate, they knew he had a 2,000-acre estate and drank good bourbon; they just wanted to cash in on the frontier appeal established by Andrew Jackson. Such symbols, from Grant's cigar stub to Al Smith's brown derby, all had a touch of the calculated.

But there is a difference between using these devices and the ways of modern political management firms. The oldtimers may sometimes have laughed up their sleeves at the emblems they used, but they did believe in the men those emblems stood for. They backed candidates for public office, not clients; and if they were often moved by hope of reward, they were just as often moved by loyalty and conviction. As these earthy amateurs are supplanted by technicians who shift from side to side, selling political proficiency for cash, elections are being robbed of some of their true meaning.

What Do You Think?

With which of the two views concerning advertising agencies presented in this reading would you agree? Why? Can you offer any further evidence to support or refute either of these views?

ACTIVITIES FOR INVOLVEMENT

1.   Listed below is the Code of Ethics of the American Association of Advertising Agencies:

We, the members of the American Association of Advertising Agencies, in addition to supporting and obeying the laws and legal regulations pertaining to advertising, undertake to extend and broaden the application of high standards. Specifically, we will not knowingly produce advertising which contains:

a. False or misleading statements or exaggerations, visual or verbal.
b. Testimonials which do not reflect the real choice of a competent witness.
c. Price claims which are misleading.
d. Comparisons which unfairly disparage a competitive product or service.
e. Claims insufficiently supported, or which distort the true meaning of practicable application of statements made by professional or scientific authority.

With the code in mind, listen to television commercials and read advertisements in magazines and newspapers in order to determine how carefully the code is followed. Make a list of any claims which violate one or more of the provisions listed in the code. Then compare your list with your classmates. What might be done about such violations?

2.   Hold a class discussion on what an ideal code of ethics should include. Then form a number of working committees to prepare drafts of such a code. Compare and contrast each committee's draft and then draw up a final statement. How would you enforce such a code?

3.   Do you feel that political commercials on television influence people in the way they vote? Do you feel that candidates for political office should be "packaged and peddled like soap"? Construct a questionnaire that would find out what influences go into how a person votes and then poll your community. (For example, you might try to determine if short TV spot commercials are remembered by more people than half-hour political programs.) Then poll the members of the class and compare your two lists. What similarities and differences do you notice? What conclusions can you draw from the results of your questionnaire as to how political advertising affects the voting habits of people?

4.   A slogan is a short, catchy phrase or sentence intended for general consumption and often designed to terminate thought and promote action in favor of the slogan maker. With this definition in mind, make a list of advertising slogans that you feel are successful and a list of slogans that you feel are unsuccessful. What makes a successful slogan? Make a list of political slogans used by a candidate or political party in past campaigns. Which ones would you say were most successful? Why? Do political slogans persuade people? Explain.

5.   Start a collection of campaign buttons or slogans and see how many different kinds there are. Try to find ones that take opposite points of view.

6.   Invite the editor of the newspaper in your community to talk to the class about advertising. Prepare ahead of time to ask such questions as:

    a. What kinds of advertising do you accept?

    b. What kinds of advertising will you not accept? Why not?

    c. How important is advertising to your newspaper?

    d. To what extent can an advertiser influence what your newspaper prints?

7.   Hold a class discussion on the topic: "High school newspapers should include advertisements."

5

Opinions, Polls, and Candidates

According to Voltaire, "Opinion has caused more trouble on this little earth than plagues or earthquakes." In the United States public opinion is given every chance to reveal itself, possibly by expressing one's thoughts to one's Congressman or writing a letter to the opinion column of the local newspaper. Many different people and groups, hoping to persuade people to their particular point of view, try to create or change public opinion through the mass media. Professional public opinion poll organizations are constantly measuring public opinion and publishing or selling privately the results. Recently these public opinion poll takers have come into question, and the United States Congress is investigating their methods in gathering and interpreting the results of their polls. In this chapter we will look at what "opinions" are, how they are formed, and how they are measured.

1. WHAT ARE OPINIONS ABOUT? *

Just how is public opinion created? What force and impact does it have on events? These are some of the questions you should look for in this reading.

Government policy, and, indeed, all important historical events, are shaped by the opinions of the members of the political communities

* Excerpted from Robert E. Land and David O. Sears, *Public Opinion* (Foundations of Modern Political Science Series). © 1964. Reprinted by permission of Prentice-Hall, Inc. Englewood Cliffs, N. J.

involved. That is why we are interested in public opinion. Shall the national government pass a civil rights bill? Have the "warhawks" prepared us for war? Shall the city issue bonds to pay for a new school? The resolution of all of these issues is influenced in one way or another by the sentiments of the public—although the influence is often circuitous and hard to follow.

PUBLIC OPINION

Opinions have to be *about* something; the ones we are mainly interested in are about four things. First, they are about the political system, the regime, the constitutional framework, the way issues get decided. These opinions get to the root of things; disagreement on such matters can, if they are widespread, cause the system to break down. One of the main functions of public opinion in a going, stable regime is to provide a generalized support for the regime. Popular opinion provides effective legitimacy. Where this legitimacy is missing, the alienation of the disaffected can be expressed in (a) apathy and withdrawal—the more usual form—or, on occasion, in (b) the special politics of alienation—often destructive, irrational . . . and seemingly less interested in *what* is to be decided than in *who* will decide. Generalized support or alienated disaffection? This is the first question for public opinion and the first reason to be interested in it.

If, as in the United States, the question of the constitutional order is pretty well agreed upon by most people, a second subject for public opinion, in our consideration, is the question of the choice of group loyalties and identifications. Opinions cluster by groups: regional, national origin, race, religion, urban-rural status, and social class or status. Consciously or unconsciously people tend to identify with such groups as these (and many more specific ones: unions, trade associations, sporting clubs, and so forth) and to draw their opinions from these identifications. Politically, one of the most important of these group loyalties is loyalty to a political party. It is derived, in part, from sentiments toward the various social groups. And party loyalty is in many ways the most important single determinant of vote decisions in the United States. Although party loyalties have a life of their own, in the long run they are likely to be determined by whether the various social groups, which are more intimately related to people's daily lives, support one or another party. The pattern of loyalties to parties and other groups, then, is a crucial focus in the study of public opinion, for it affects the broadest policy orientations of government, gives strength to some group demands and not others, and directly affects the choice of leaders.

The choice of leaders itself is a third area of public opinion which attracts our attention. The public makes its selection only after the field has been narrowed down to a few of the many possible candidates, but the narrowing down is obviously done with public reaction in mind—and the final estimate by the public in its role as electorate is an important one. What kind of men do various elements of the public prefer? Strong, heroic types . . . ? Men with certain "common-man" qualities whose reactions will be familiar and understood? Men whose social and occupational status makes it appropriate that they should hold "high office"? Public preferences and opinions on these matters shape public policy and the course of history in a variety of important ways.

Finally (fourth) there is the matter of public issues—topics, like the civil rights legislation mentioned above, or admission of China to the United Nations, or an embargo on Cuba, or aid to education by the federal government—on which some segment of the public has an opinion. These topics vary greatly in their power to attract attention and support of opposition; often the attentive public is rather small, and the informed public even smaller, but in the absence of strong opposition even a small public can make its influence felt. On the other hand, there is often a diffuse, badly informed, but intensely held set of opinions prevalent among a large public, a situation which poses a hazard for the better-informed political leaders. However these qualities of interest, intensity, and persuasion may be distributed, the issues which the course of history throws to the surface at any one time will find a resolution somehow shaped by public opinion.

TRANSLATING OPINION INTO POLICY

The process of "shaping" is an enormously complicated one, but at the very least we can identify, if not completely explain, some of the ways in which this is done. The most obvious, of course, is the electoral process culminating in the vote. Here the ordinary members of the public . . . experience a sense of choice and, for the most part, a feeling of influencing important events. Beyond that, there is the matter of writing letters and sending deputations to Congress or the State House or some other seat of power. Only about 10 per cent of the American public in any one year undertake this kind of activity. The act of joining, and therefore supporting, one or more of the many overlapping "interest-groups" in the United States gives force to some points of view, sometimes a point of view explicitly presented to civil servants and legislatures by lobbyists. This is also true, in a less obvious way, of the support given to certain media. Congressmen pay a great deal of attention to what the papers and television and radio commentators are saying. Papers with a wide circulation and programs with a considerable audience are, in a sense, made more powerful by their audiences. Then, too, there is the survey or poll respondent whose answers to questions on issues and men become part of a news report (or perhaps a private research report to the sponsoring official) revealing the current state of opinion . . .

What Do You Think?

1.   What kind of opinions are discussed in this reading? How
would you define an opinion at this point?
2.   The author states that only 10 per cent of the American
public write their Congressmen. How would you explain this?

2.   WHAT IS AN OPINION? *

*A person with very little knowledge may have very strong opinions.
Why might this be so?*

Miss Sherwin of Gopher Prairie, says Walter Lippmann, is trying to understand the news reports on the First World War. "She has never been
to France, and certainly she has never been along what is now the battle-
front. Pictures of French and German soldiers she has seen, but it is
impossible for her to imagine three million men. . . . Miss Sherwin has
no access to the order of battle maps, and so if she is to think about the
war, she fastens upon Joffre [the general in command of the French Forces
in WW I] and the Kaiser as if they were engaged in a personal duel."

[An interviewer] asked O'Hara, a sprightly little mechanic in East-
port, "What groups do you think have the most influence on city politics?"
First he frowned and then he smiled: "Oh (pause) labor has something
to do with it—there's no doubt about that; your Knights of Columbus,
your Masons, and things like that. They've got a lot to do with it, because,
as it is, the higher you get up in the Knights, or you get up in the Masons
or something, you're more or less up there—you're pulling a lot more
weight there. Your veterans' organizations have a lot to do with it, too—
like your American Legion and that. The American Legion has a lot to
do with it, not only in the city, but all over—they pull a lot of power."
O'Hara is a lot closer to the city politics than Miss Sherwin is to the
battlefronts, but like her, he must pull together a lot of vague impressions,
organize them, and formulate an opinion.

An opinion, we will say, is "an implicit verbal response or 'answer'
that an individual gives in response to a particular stimulus situation in
which some general 'question' is raised." It may or may not be overtly
expressed; [the interviewer] asked O'Hara to express his opinions, but

* Excerpted from Robert E. Land and David O. Sears, *Public Opinion* (Foundations of Modern Political Science Series). © 1964. Reprinted by permission
of Prentice-Hall, Inc. Englewood Cliffs, N. J.

perhaps he had a private opinion on the power of these groups before it came up in this way and perhaps he had some opinions he did not care to tell his interviewer. In reading the paper Miss Sherwin may have been formulating opinions which she never had a chance to express. But if they are expressed, or implied, so that an analyst can see them, how shall we describe them?

DESCRIBING AN OPINION

The two dimensions which public opinion analysts most commonly use to describe an opinion are *direction* and *intensity*.

Direction:

When we say an opinion has direction, we mean that it includes some affective, or emotional, quality of approving or disapproving of something. It has a "pro con" quality. Miss Sherwin is pro-Joffre and anti-Kaiser in their duel. Stated or implied, this pro con quality is almost always there.

If direction tells us, in effect, "yes" or "no," what shall we do with "maybe" or "it depends"? There are, in effect, requests by the respondent for new "questions" with greater specificity so that he may qualify his commitment, avoiding a "yes" or "no" answer. This is the purpose of a "qualified answer." . . .

Some groups of people tend to qualify answers more than others: Educated people give more "qualified" answers than do those with little education; and intensity of feeling, as one might expect, tends to discourage qualification. Oral answers, too, tend to bring out qualifications more than do written communications. Qualifications serve something of a protective function in the face-to-face situation; also, the ease of expression tends to make the longer qualified statement less of a burden.

Under some circumstances, there are tendencies to give mostly pro or mostly con answers regardless of the content of the question. . . . In New York in 1945, in reply to queries on why persons were voting for their respective candidates (O'Dwyer, Morris, Goldstein) [an interviewer] received only vague and unpersuasive answers such as a man's "good experience" or "his good record." But this was not true of answers to queries about why people voted against the opposition candidate. Here the replies were informed and emotional, suggestion that more thought and attention went into these negative aspects of voting than went into the endorsements implied in a positive vote. . . .

In summary, then, the first thing to understand about an opinion is its direction. Both individual personality patterns and culture may produce general dispositions to give positive answers or negative answers, more or less independent of the content of the question.

Intensity:

People feel very strongly about certain of their opinions, much less strongly about others. Thus, in inquiring about their opinions it makes sense to ask people to specify the intensity of their feeling. For example, in 1956 the Survey Research Center presented its respondents with the following statement: "The government ought to help people get doctors and hospital care at low cost." And it asked them to reply in these terms: "agree strongly, agree not very strongly, not sure, it depends, disagree but not very strongly, disagree strongly." The first and last are of course the most intense responses.

Intensity is also an important dimension of loyalty to groups. After asking people to report which party they generally favored, the SRC interviewers asked them: "Would you call yourself a strong (Republican) (Democrat) or a not very strong (Republican) (Democrat)?" In general people do not have much trouble stating how strongly they feel about opinions of these kinds. . . .

INFORMATIONAL CONTENT

As everyone knows, there are informed opinions and uninformed opinions. [It has been observed] that "information support" does not refer so much to the opinion itself as "the amount of the available information that may go into the building of" the opinion, but the two are so closely allied, they should be treated together. One of the most interesting aspects of opinion on public affairs is the degree to which people will hold rather "strong" views on matters on which they have almost no information; the intensity of opinion coming from some symbol, such as "flag," or the word "Constitution," or from some reference group, such as "Irish" or "southerner," rather than from a reasoned view of probable consequences of a course of action.

One of the criteria of an informed opinion is the degree of *differentiation* employed; that is, the discrimination among events or people or issues in a way relevant to the opinion. The lumping together of all forms of government enterprise (Post Office, public irrigation, TVA) as "creeping socialism" or the stereotyping of all Negroes in a single bundle of traits represent the failure of differentiation. A person with a highly differentiated opinion is usually more aware of alternative responses.

A second kind of information is the awareness of the *implications* of an opinion. Polls have shown that almost everyone supports the idea of free speech, but few people understand that this implies granting people who hold positions they particularly dislike the right to speak. Thus [one] study [found that] more than a third of the respondents would deny the right of free speech for "someone who wanted to speak in this city against churches and religion." Under these circumstances one would say that those who supported the idea of free speech and the Bill of Rights, but denied its implications, were uninformed. . . . The great discrepancy between what seems to be expected of the public and what it is in fact capable of doing raises considerable doubts, not about democracy, which seems fairly healthy in America, but about our theory of the representative process.

Another important characteristic of an opinion cluster is its degree of organization. First, the degree of *integration* or *isolation* of various opinions is often important. The extreme ideologue may have a set of opinions all of which are continually referred one to another. A citizen with poorly organized opinions may, on the other hand, hold several which are clearly relevant to each other, but which he has never thought of in connection with each other.

A second significant characteristic of an opinion cluster is the notion of *breadth*. One might ask for example, whether prejudice toward Negroes is an exception to a generally tolerant view of other people or, as is more likely, is a part of a broad ethnocentrism: the tendency to reject others ethnically not like oneself. The study called *The Authoritarian Personality,* by Adorno and others, showed that anti-Semitism was often part of a broadly ethnocentric view of others. This study also revealed that prejudiced people have an even more general tendency first to sort out people into an admired in-group and a disliked out-group and second to assign a "higher" or a "lower" place to everyone so that the world appeared as a kind of general status hierarchy.

Finally, in this explication of "organization" there is Lazarsfeld's idea of "frame of reference." Within what scheme of values, he asks, is an opinion held? For example, in Lewin's study of diet changes during World War II—a study which revealed that only when a person achieved a certain economic security did he view diet as a matter of health more than a matter of budget—opinions on diet were influenced by such values as money or health.

The organization of an opinion cluster has a great deal to do with the problem of rationality. . . .

CONSISTENCY

One reason why people hold inconsistent opinions is that they have different opinions for different social situations. According to the definition of an opinion given earlier, an opinion is an "answer" that is given to "a question" in a given situation. When the question *or* situation varies somewhat, a somewhat different response can be expected. Differences in the wording of questions often give quite different results, as the following examples show. In June, 1941, when asked whether they favored the United States entering the war against Germany and Italy or staying out, 29 per cent of one sample of the public said that they favored American entry. But when a similar sample was asked this question with several other options, such as supplying Britain with war materials, only 6 per cent favored entering the war against Germany and Italy (American Institute of Public Opinion, May, 1941). What is the "true" opinion? The question makes no sense because the alternatives brought to the attention of the respondents are different in each case. Similar findings were reported by Payne in a study of attitudes toward public health insurance. He found that in one poll in which a sample was asked its opinion on extending the social security laws to cover doctor and hospital care, 68 per cent of the sample supported this idea. When another similar sample was asked if it favored medical insurance supported by the private insurance companies, 70 per cent of the respondents supported *this* idea. Finally, when a sample was forced to choose between the two positions, 35 per cent favored governmental medical insurance, and 31 per cent favored private medical insurance, with the remainder either indifferent or not offering an opinion.

THE POLICY COMPONENT

The problem of inconsistencies in a person's opinions on a given topic, stemming from differences in stimulus situations, comes up most frequently in connection with discrepancies between verbally expressed opinions and action. A person may express one opinion verbally (e.g., Negroes should be allowed to live where they please) but not behave consistent with that opinion (e.g., actively oppose a Negro's moving in next door). One's analysis of such inconsistencies depends upon one's view of opinions generally. . . .

Some kinds of opinions seem "actionable" while others are not. Cantril says, in reference to opinions during World War II: "Opinions upon which concrete judgments and actions are based, often appear to go contrary to opinions abstractly held, since the latter are purely intellectual data that either call for no concrete action or offer no possibility of concrete action. An example of the difference between an abstract opinion and an opinion guiding behavior is presented in La Piere's now classic and rather simple study. He traveled throughout the United States with a Chinese couple, stopping at 66 sleeping places and 184 eating places. On only one occasion were the Chinese couple refused service. At the conclusion of the trip, La Piere sent a questionnaire to the proprietors of these hostelries asking if they would accept members of the Chinese race as their patrons. He received negative replies from 92 per cent of the sleeping places and 93 per cent of the eating places.

What Do You Think?

1.   How would you define an opinion now?
2.   Which of your own opinions do you feel very strongly about? Why?

3.   It has been suggested that opinions are efforts to "oppose or accomplish something." Would you agree? Why or why not? Cite examples in support of your reasoning.

3.   HOW POLLSTERS MAKE OR BREAK CANDIDATES *

Next, we see how potent a force political polls have become.

WEIGHING THE WAYS OF GALLUP, HARRIS AND ASSOCIATES

When a major candidate for the Republican Presidential nomination withdraws from the race before he has faced a single primary election, as Michigan Gov. George Romney did [in 1968], he must feel certain what the voters' decision would be. There is only one basis for him and his advisors to make such a judgment: polls.

The Romney decision illustrates how potent a force political polling has become in American life. But its impact is no surprise to the increasing number of sophisticated politicians who are relying ever more strongly on what the polls tell them.

Polls have been laughed at often enough in the past—like the one that said Alf Landon would defeat Franklin D. Roosevelt in 1936 or the ones that predicted a Thomas E. Dewey victory over Harry S. Truman in 1948. They are by no means perfect now, and many persons remain doubtful. But the men who understand polls best—not the pollsters, who make their living this way, but the politicians who need them as a tool—are, in effect, staking their careers on them. . . .

Governor Romney has unusual faith in them, perhaps partly the result of his experience with market research when he was president of American Motors. His use of polls is credited with helping him achieve his three victories in Michigan gubernatorial races and, especially, with the successful drives he led to elect Sen. Robert Griffin and five underdog Republican congressional candidates in 1966.

THE NATION'S LEADER

Says one astute political observer: "The Romney organization in Michigan is incontestably the nation's leader in the art of political polling."

The man who has conducted Mr. Romney's polls since 1962 is Fred Currier, through his firm, Market Opinion Research of Detroit. . . . Governor Romney saw the raw data from the third extensive poll Mr. Currier

---

* Excerpted from James R. Dickenson, "How Pollsters Make or Break Candidates—Weighing the Ways of Gallup, Harris, and Associates." *The National Observer,* July 19, 1968.

had taken in New Hampshire. The result: Nixon 70.3 per cent; Romney 11.5 per cent; Nelson Rockefeller (write-in) 8.4 per cent; others (write-in) 5.0; undecided 4.8.

Now, no public poll stands alone. Each is—in the language of the experts—a bench mark. A good poll represents, with a margin of error of perhaps 3 per cent, what the people think at a static period in time—how a hypothetical election at that moment would have turned out.

However, good polls, considered as a series, can show trends and ups and downs. Once, after all, Governor Romney led everyone at the polls. Governor Rockefeller . . . was making a charge in the polls; then he leveled off or fell back.

That is what made the showing of Governor Romney in New Hampshire so distressing to the governor. In all the three "waves" of extensive polling, there was never a variance of more than two to three points. "The fascinating thing," says a top aide of the governor's, "is that we couldn't seem to move it."

Mr. Currier's operation on behalf of Mr. Romney is one of the many private polls being conducted constantly for politicians. The public seldom hears their results, except when politicians want it to; but the public is affected by them because they help guide the politicians on how to convince the public.

The polls that everyone does hear about, and that many people interested in politics try to interpret, are the "public polls," which are reported weekly in the press.

Without these heavily publicized polls—and the Gallup and Harris polls are the most publicized—no one would have a scientific yardstick to measure the changing attitudes of the voters. In the old days, instinct sufficed, because it had to. Now, with polls becoming more and more accepted because, in fact, they are becoming more accurate and scientific, rationality becomes a substitute for seat-of-the-pants instinct.

Political polling is becoming a big business. A few years ago, there were a handful of political pollsters; now there are 200 to 300 of them. Gallup and Harris stand almost alone because they are public pollsters, which means that they publish their findings for their clients for profit. Neither the Gallup nor the Harris organizations works for private clients.

If the accuracy of polling—at least that polling done by recognized, expert professionals—is no longer seriously questioned, the impact that polls have on politicians themselves and the voters generally is still very much a point of debate. . . .

BANDWAGON THEORY

While they are agreed on the polls' influence on politicians, the pollsters are much less eager to talk about their effect on voter behavior, a concern of many laymen. George Gallup insists there is no such thing as a "bandwagon" effect in which voters see a candidate leading in the polls and decide to back a winner. Mr. Harris, who made his reputation as John F. Kennedy's private pollster in 1960 and now is Mr. Gallup's rival as a national, public pollster, concurs: "My argument, and it's unanswerable as far as I can see, is that if there were any so-called 'bandwagon effect' there would be no such thing as a wrong poll, and there have been plenty of them." Richard Nixon, he points out, began the 1960 Presidential campaign leading John F. Kennedy in the polls.

There are those, however, who make a distinction between the impact of polls in primary as against general elections. In primaries, the voters are usually all from one party and many of them are loyal members of the party. Such people often tend to look for a winner. If the polls show a man they can relate to coming up, they may join him in his climb. Many people believe this is precisely what happened in the New Hampshire Presidential primary in 1964, when Henry Cabot Lodge swept to victory in the closing hours of the campaign, *after* the pollsters had detected a groundswell for him.

Many people agree, too, that polls have an impact on voter turnout. If the polls show a winner, it is argued, some voters may decide that there's no point in bothering to vote. . . .

As unwelcome as this question is, the pollsters can at least take comfort in the fact that it indicates an increased acceptance of their reliability. The polls have come a long way since George Gallup, Elmo Roper, and Archibald Crossley pioneered the techniques of modern polling in 1935.

That was at a time when the business of measuring public opinion was conducted primarily by the Literary Digest, whose polls predicting election outcomes had become famous. In 1936, however, disaster struck. The Literary Digest predicted that Alf Landon would defeat Franklin Roosevelt with 57 per cent of the vote. Instead, the Kansas governor got only 37.5 per cent and carried only two states (inspiring the famous quip that, "As goes Maine, so goes Vermont").

The problem was that the Digest's findings were based on a sampling of telephone users and automobile owners—in those Depression days the marks of the more affluent voters, who tended to oppose FDR's economic and social programs. The Gallup Poll warned its newspaper clients that the Digest poll was going to be wrong, and why.

Twelve years later Gallup and Roper understood how the Literary Digest editors felt. Most of the opinion pollsters predicted that Thomas Dewey would defeat Harry Truman. The primary mistake they made was that they stopped polling too early; Gallup's last poll, on Oct. 15, was 18 days before the election, and thus didn't pick up the late swing to

Truman among the undecided, Midwest farmers, and disillusioned Henry Wallace supporters. Another source of error was superficial questions that didn't reveal intensity of voter feeling on issues and candidates.

Since 1948, however, the pollsters have avoided major disasters, and business has flourished.

The greatest increase is in the number of poll takers who do private studies for politicians. . . .

There are . . . good ones . . . and many incompetents; anyone who wants to can hang out a shingle and call himself a poll taker. But as diverse as they are, there is one thing that good ones have in common: the concern that their "sample"—the people they select for questioning— is drawn scientifically so that it accurately reflects public opinion in the "universe," the area (it can be the entire nation, a state, a city, or con- gressional district) they want to measure.

The procedure for drawing a sample is based on the statistical law of probability, which for the poll taker's purpose means that each in- dividual in the area to be measured must have an exactly equal chance of being selected. The selection must be entirely at random. A simple example of this is to have a complete, up-to-date list of all registered voters. If there are, say, 1,000 registered voters and the researcher picks every 50th name, he will have a random sample of 20 that will be repre- sentative of the whole.

The idea is to leave everything to chance, with no human selection. At the block level a starting point is arbitrarily picked and the interviewer proceeds from there on strict instructions, either every subsequent house or every fourth house or something like that (Gallup will never start with corner houses because they tend to be somewhat more affluent, but if a corner house turns up in the normal subsequent interval, it is included). The interviewer is given instructions as to whom to interview, the oldest male voter in one house, say, the youngest female voter in the next, the youngest male next, and so on.

Many laymen are doubtful that a sample of 1,500 people can ac- curately reflect the views of 200,000,000 people, but if they are selected strictly at random such a sample is ordinarily sufficient. The increase in accuracy of a larger sample generally isn't enough to justify the added cost (about $10 per interview), although Mr. Harris will sample 4,800 people just before an election. The normal sample size guarantees a 95 per cent chance that he will be within 3 percentage points of the actual division of opinion. This means, of course, that in a very close election, such as 1960 when John F. Kennedy got 50.1 per cent of the vote, it's still possible to pick the wrong man.

Accuracy of the sample is more important than size; the 1936 Liter- ary Digest prediction was based on 2,375,000 returns. If a sample is bad, making it larger won't help. The major criticism statisticians make of the pollsters' sampling is that if no one is home at one of the selected houses, the interviewer goes on to another. Because of the cost involved, they don't try to call back, and this, according to statisticians, means that those who are frequently away from home have less chance to be interviewed. The Gallup Poll, in an effort to offset this, asks each respondent how many times in the previous three days he was home at the hour of the interview; the fewer times, Gallup figures, the greater the chance that he represents a not-at-home, and the interview is weighted accordingly.

It is not how the information is gathered, however, that is subject to most questioning, but how it's interpreted. Lou Harris is a frequent target of criticism by his colleagues (as jealous and backbiting as any group of academics or opera divas) for—they say—overinterpreting and drawing conclusions the data don't support. Mr. Harris, on the other hand, thinks many of his critics irresponsibly throw out undigested and therefore meaningless raw data to the public. . . .

A SOURCE OF INTELLIGENCE

If used as a source of intelligence and information, [private] polls can be useful. To ignore them can be damaging; one of Mr. Nixon's 1960 campaign managers insists that if he had heeded his confidential poll that showed Illinois evenly divided and campaigned intensively there, Mr. Nixon might have carried the state—and the election. Instead he went to Alaska.

There are times when polls are no help and a politician has to rely on his instincts, which is what really separates the good politicians from the bad. John F. Kennedy's dramatic intervention in behalf of Martin Luther King in 1960 is a good example; he made the decision immediately and instinctively, and it probably won him a good share of the Northern urban Negro vote that helped win the election.

But there is hardly a politician alive who would not like to be told, scientifically, that his instincts are good (or bad) politics. And that's why there is talk about the simulator, a technique employing a high-speed computer filled with bits and pieces from old polls. Some day, the experts say, the simulator will be able to give immediate answers on what the public will think about an event that hasn't even occurred.

When that day comes, politicians will be spared the danger of taking steps in the dark. The voters may or may not be more enlightened.

What Do You Think?

1.   Suppose you were being interviewed by a newspaper reporter from a foreign country. How would you explain to him why political candidates believe polls to be so important?

2.   Why do politicians consider polls so important? If the polls show a politician losing, should he withdraw from the race or should he fight harder to win? What would you do? Explain.

4. THE ABUSES AND FEARS OF POLLING POWER *

Here is another view of the power of polls. Compare it with the reading just preceding. What differences do you notice?

There are about 200 different polls going in the country today and there is almost no agreement among them as to the best way to conduct a poll. They disagree on what constitutes the proper size of a sampling. They have no standardized interviewing technique. There are a dozen different kinds of polls—house-to-house polls, telephone polls, TV polls, postcard polls, coupon polls, newspaper polls, street-corner polls. The public, understandably confused, shows a rather wide skepticism as to their worth. A poll on polls taken by the Minneapolis *Tribune* revealed that 45 per cent of those interviewed did not think a survey could be accurate if based on only 2,000 interviews, hundreds more than pollsters normally use.

The major pollsters do go about their work carefully, sensibly, but differently. The two major public polls, Gallup and Harris, operate under contrasting philosophies. "We're just fact finders," says Dr. Gallup, who limits himself largely to percentage breakdowns with little interpretation when he takes a reading of an issue or a candidate. But Lou Harris insists on doing some interpretation. On the issue of gun control, for example, Gallup concluded his most recent survey by stating simply that 85 per cent of the public wants registration of hand guns. Harris went further. He found that 81 per cent wanted control but 61 per cent wanted to be allowed to own arms themselves—thus indicating that the public was not as single-minded as the Gallup percentage suggested. "It's digging beneath the surface to find out what people think that is the obligation of public opinion research," says Harris.

Gallup and Harris do no private polling for candidate or political parties. There are dozens of pollsters who do. They try to find out what voters like and don't like about a candidate and look for issues that should be exploited—or avoided. The classic case of a private poll's value came in 1960 when Lou Harris—then a private pollster—looked into the troublesome Catholic issue for John F. Kennedy. He found so much suspicion of Kennedy's religion, so many half-believed rumors about it,

---

* Excerpted from John Pekkanen, "The Abuses and Fears of Polling Power," *Life* Magazine, July 19, 1968. © 1968 Time, Inc.

that he recommended bringing the whole thing out into the open. Kennedy did and blunted religion as a campaign issue.

The private polls, since they are for hire and are not open to public scrutiny, are the most susceptible to manipulation and abuse. The most flagrant recent episode occurred . . . when sources in the Johnson administration leaked word that a private poll had found the President standing much better with the voters than either Harris or Gallup showed. The poll, it was said, proved Johnson was ahead of potential Republican opposition in New York and Pennsylvania and was leading four Republican opponents in an unnamed "bellwether county" in New Hampshire.

The poll, it turned out, was conducted for Arthur B. Krim, a backer of the President, by Archibald Crossley. Crossley is a highly respected private pollster, but what was leaked to the press represented only a portion of his survey. The "bellwether county" was Democratic and one in which Johnson had received a much higher percentage of the vote in 1964 than he had nationwide. In New York, where Johnson was reported to have run well, the leaked figures did not match him against Governor Rockefeller, the strongest potential opponent there. Crossley was so angered at the leak that he himself gave out the poll's real findings.

In a large eastern state a few years ago, a group of politicians, anxious to run their candidate, commissioned a poll whose results would inevitably favor their man. Then they showed the results, in strict confidence, to party leaders—who spread the word to county chairmen and delegates. A well-timed leak to the press whipped up wider enthusiasm. The candidate was nominated—then trounced in the election. . . .

Within the industry there is now a concerted effort to curb the use of polls for such tactical purposes or for sheer abuse. The American Association for Public Opinion Research, to which nearly all leading pollsters belong, this spring adopted a set of standards to draw the line between scientifically conducted polls, and "those which reflect an ignorance of or willful unconcern with good research practice." The standards demand that the public—or in the case of a private poll, the client—be apprised of the methods used in obtaining poll results.

These standards closely parallel a "truth in polling" bill . . . introduced into the House of Representatives by Congressman Lucien Nedzi of Detroit. His bill required that data on a poll be filed in the Library of Congress within 72 hours after it has been made public—such facts as the size of the sample, the time the poll was taken, the questions asked and the places canvassed. "Obviously," says Nedzi, "you can get the kind of results you want by going to a particular place, like going to any Army base to get opinions on the Vietnam war. And polls are inevitably opinion-forming as well as fact-finding."

Dr. Gallup, a strong advocate of polling ethics, says of the Nedzi bill: "There are many things that are done in the name of polling and half of them are guaranteed to get the wrong answers. I think we need this legislation." But Harris finds the bill "an abridgement of the freedom of inquiry and the freedom of reporting." Burns Roper, head of Roper Research Associates, hopes the problem can be solved without federal legislation "but I'm not sure it can be." Thus a poll of the pollsters brings the full range of classic responses: one for, one against, one don't know.

Harris contends that the problem of disclosure is "10 years out of date." "It's been solved," he says flatly. There is a more complex and basic problem to be faced—the "horrible prospect" of a political candidate winning an election and exercising power only by consensus.

This problem cannot be dismissed, as it is among some pollsters, by the bland assertion that politicians have been seeking consensus since the days of Machiavelli. The massive brain-picking of the electorate by pollsters will more clearly than ever define just what the consensus is and it will require greater acts of political courage to ignore the consensus. Dr. Gallup argues that the public is "months, sometimes decades ahead of the legislative leaders." But consensus does lag behind policies. For example: opinion polls on a nuclear testban treaty taken before it was signed in 1963 showed the public against any such treaty. The public changed its mind, however, after the treaty was signed and it had been educated to its importance.

The public, says Harris, is woefully backward in understanding the country's most crucial domestic issue, the race crisis. The "jaws of consent," he insists, are not wide enough to encompass all the radical ideas essential to solving it. "If you're running this country," he says, "you won't be able to solve the race crisis and remain popular."

The poll-gotten solution is not necessarily the right one—and a politician's success in the long run depends on how courageously he resists the temptation to forego leadership to play the percentages of the pollsters.

What Do You Think?

1. After reading the last two articles, how would you describe polls? Explain.
2. Would you endorse a truth-in-polling bill as suggested? Why or why not?
3. Would you advocate abolishing polls? Why or why not?

5. RATE YOUR CANDIDATE *

One kind of poll is to find out how Congressmen feel about a particular topic. Here are some of the questions sent to Congressmen to

---

* Excerpted from Michael Frome, "Rate Your Candidate," *Field & Stream,* September 1968.

find out their attitudes about conservation. After the Congressmen answered the poll their names were published as friends or enemies of conservation. Would this poll have any influence on you?

1. LAND AND WATER CONSERVATION FUND
   Amounts available to the Fund have proven inadequate to finance new National Parks, Seashores, and Recreation Areas; to purchase National Forest in-holdings; and to match state expenditures for expanding outdoor facilities.
   > Do you favor an adequate program of financing acquisition of new areas and in-holdings?   YES __ NO __
   > Did you vote yes to earmarking Outer Continental Shelf mineral revenues for this purpose (as all conservation organizations urged)?   YES __ NO __

2. ESTUARINE AREAS
   Tidal marshes, shallow sounds, and coastal bays where the rivers meet the sea provide immensely valuable habitat for birds, waterfowl, mammals, and fish. Yet thousands of miles are being destroyed by dredging, filling, oil exploration, and garbage dumping.
   > Do you support the Estuaries Act to inventory all estuaries, establish Federal, state and local plans to conserve and restore areas suited for wildlife and recreation?   YES __ NO __

3. MANAGEMENT OF PUBLIC LANDS
   Large-scale disposal of public lands started fading in the 1920's. But only in 1964 did Congress move to provide adequate management on lands to be retained in public ownership. In 1968 it voted to extend the Classification and Multiple Use Act an additional three years.
   > Did you vote yes for original passage and later extension of the act?   YES __ NO __
   > Do you support present classification activities of the Bureau of Land Management?   YES __ NO __
   > Do you favor multiple-use management of public lands for watershed, wildlife, and recreation, as well as for commercial uses?
   >   YES __ NO __

4. WILDERNESS PROTECTION
   The Wilderness Law of 1964 provides for Congressional action on individual Federal areas for inclusion in the National Wilderness Preservation System.
   > Are you prepared to support enactment of legislation establishing the many wilderness areas in National Forests. National Parks, and National Wildlife Refuges?   YES __ NO __
   > Do you endorse preservation of wilderness by executive action in areas administered by the BLM, as provided in the Classification and Multiple Use Act?   YES __ NO __

5. **REDWOOD NATIONAL PARK**
   Congress finally came to grips with the need to save the last majestic forests of these ancient coastal monarchs. Timber companies, however, demanded a trade-off of National Forest land for their holdings, threatening a dangerous precedent which could be repeated anywhere.

   Did you support a large, adequate park?   YES ___ NO ___
   Did you oppose National Forest sacrifice?   YES ___ NO ___

6. **PORK BARREL BOONDOGGLES**
   Self-propelled construction agencies, like the U. S. Army Corps of Engineers, Tennessee Valley Authority, and Bureau of Reclamation, exert great influence in Congress with promises of pouring funds into Congressional districts in order to dam free-flowing rivers and destroy their natural values.

   Are you opposed to damming such streams as:
   the Big South Fork of the Cumberland in Tennessee, which ranks among the most scenic?   YES ___ NO ___
   the vital Clearwater in Idaho?   YES ___ NO ___
   the Salmon in Idaho, the longest stream in the West still free of dams?   YES ___ NO ___
   Are you sponsoring a similar reservoir project in your own area that would skyrocket land values for the benefit of real estate boomers?   YES ___ NO ___

What Do You Think?

1. What effect might a poll like this have on Congressmen? Why?
2. Is this polling effort an example of propaganda?

6.   AND WHAT IS TELEVISION'S INFLUENCE? *

Now that you have some idea of what an opinion is, we can begin to gain an idea of how opinions are formed. First, we look at television and its influence in electing political candidates.

What ICBM's have done to the military world, what computers have done to the business world, what jets and supersonic planes have done to the aviation world—so much has television done to the political campaign world. TV is just as new, hits just as hard, moves just as fast.

---

* Excerpted from Herbert M. Baus and William B. Ross, *Politics Battle Plan*, New York, N. Y.: The Macmillan Company, 1968.

TV has upset centuries of accumulated traditions just as much. The future of TV is just as exciting. TV's potential for good *and* for evil is just as great. And, compared with the puny price of doing the accustomed things the old-fashioned way, TV's costs are just as astronomical.

TV brings the action directly to the viewer. It is instantaneous, it is personal, it is completely realistic. It is direct communication often staged and embellished for a desired effect, but pure and basic, virtually person to person.

"Newspapers try to transmit facts," said John Chancellor, former Voice of America Director, as quoted in *Time*. "Television is the transmission of experience in its rawest form."

Commentator Howard K. Smith summarized, "Television is not just a picture medium. It is pictures, plus words, plus personality."

Television has revolutionized campaign style, rewritten campaign strategy, skyrocketed campaign costs, fantastically increased candidate contact with more people—and made it easier for Fickle Fate to flip political fortunes with a flick of her finger.

Weighing the premium television puts on a candidate's looks, his voice, his clothes, and his stage presence leads serious thinkers to question its ultimate impact on the quality of government. Mankind will continue to need office holders who can think, judge, decide, lead, and get things done.

Television has blown the fresh air of enormous public exposure into politics. It has vitiated to some extent the once formidable power of cigar-smoking bosses to install in office their hand-picked puppets. And it has enabled the politically unknown challenger to go all the way in a single election by outperforming a less gifted incumbent. The result is praise from those the camera and commentators favor, and caustic comment from those lacking photogenic features and friendly telecasters.

*   *   *   *   *

Many radio and television stations are making communications history by officially departing from their long years of abstention from controversy. They are forthrightly editorializing for and against the issues of the day and even endorsing candidates for office. . . .

"What might have been" had television arrived generations earlier? Television might have elected as President, Aaron Burr, a debonair ladies' man, con man, and scoundrel in preference to the comparably shy and dry Thomas Jefferson. It might have cost history the greatness of the ungainly Abraham Lincoln—although "Honest Abe," as a crowd-pleasing debater, might have conquered television as he did the Confederacy.

Henry Clay has been described . . . as "of magnificent bearing, possessing the true oratorical temperament, the nervous exaltation that makes the orator feel and appear a superior being transfusing his thought, passion, and will into the mind and heart of the listener." William Jennings Bryan was an American name synonymous with oratorical flourish. Both of these able men tried many times to become President; neither of them ever made it. Who can say how many times they might have been elected had television been available to project their declamatory prowess?

The ambitious politician who today expects to use television as a highway to high office must be a rich man or have rich friends. In 1964 the two major parties combined spent 35 million dollars on television, twice as much as they spent in 1960 and four times what they spent in 1956. This is to say nothing of concomitant costs for traveling camera crews (which can be higher than $1,000 a day) and for television consultants and creators.

With its unfathomable scope and power, television can be awesome in its potential to destroy, cruel in its quickness to maim, or overwhelming in its capacity to portray. Television is automatic and implacable in its facility to expose phonies. Any weakness or inadequacy of the candidate comes through and registers inexorably with the viewing public. While otherwise strong men and good public servants might be mortally wounded by incompetent television performance, the record also has established that articulate, photogenic political unknowns can use TV to win political wars. . . .

Taking a long look into our potential future of "government by personality" . . .

Entertainment-world candidates combine all the emerging essentials: Established name, attractive face and pleasant personality, ability to deliver a prepared talk with freshness and seeming sincerity, the poise to look at ease in silly situations. A high Nielsen rating may soon become the surest path to political nomination.

Today's multimillion-dollar TV advertising campaign budgets attest to the potency of the TV commercial—whether canned speech, glittering spot announcement, or documentary extravaganza.

But on TV, as via the press, the news or feature treatment can pack more wallop than the finest advertisement, since so many have built-in resistance to anything people identify as a paid advertisement fabricated to sell them something. Their guard is down when the message comes across as news or feature material.

The brief flash on the regular news program is the butter on the TV toast. Senator Robert F. Kennedy blithely averred that he would rather appear for thirty seconds on an evening news program than have the same story about him printed in every newspaper in the world. That was his opinion, but any astute campaign manager would rather see his candidate come on strong with thirty seconds on the evening news than with thirty minutes of canned commercial by federal law branded, "This is a paid political announcement."

The candidate to watch is the one whose manager or whose personal ubiquity can get him on such news flashes by press conferences, performances, dedication, confrontations, getting on a horse at a parade, going from station to station to march on camera at the source, or even issuing a newsworthy statement.

Los Angeles Mayor Sam Yorty, with an almost fund-free campaign, almost upset Governor Pat Brown in the 1966 California Democratic primary. He employed an interesting technique for getting on news programs.

The mayor's television news publicist would ask small town television commentators to "ask a question of Sam Yorty for your show tomorrow night."

The commentator would dream up one or two tough ones. The publicist would take his candidate into a Hollywood studio where Yorty would face the camera and give his answer. The film or tape was promptly processed and shipped to the television station, where the following night local viewers would see and hear their favorite commentator "interviewing" Mayor Yorty.

The Brown campaign leaders were dumbfounded that the peripatetic Yorty could cover so much ground, seemingly being in El Centro one night, in Crescent City 1,000 miles away the next, and sometimes in several places hundreds of miles apart the same day. Then they discovered that a television adaptation of the publicity handout was at work.

*   *   *   *   *

From as far away as Philadelphia the TV critic of that city's *Bulletin,* Rex Polier, sent up the first loud wail:

I don't care whether it materializes or not in Los Angeles. That town is Kooksville and what it does is its business. I don't like the idea of a politician in his own show which, ostensibly, is supposed to be entertainment.

In fact, he is being given the same subtle access to a powerful medium that some other personalities in America's past were given, often with sensational and undesirable results.

Philadelphia's Polier carried his direct comment on the Sam Yorty Show into a deeper commentary on the responsibilities of television in the modern political world: "TV appearances of politicians and their utterances should always be subject to the most careful considerations. It is broadcasting's solemn duty to see that their remarks and positions are sufficiently analyzed by qualified observers to make sure that whatever calculated impressions the politicians leave are not allowed to achieve permanency."

What Do You Think?

1. Do people get elected on the basis of their TV personality? How can you be sure?
2. Could a person like Abe Lincoln be elected today after the people saw him on television?
3. Would you rate television as an asset or liability to political candidates? Why?

7. THE EFFECT OF RUMOR ON POLITICAL CANDIDATES *

Have you ever been affected by rumors? This next reading suggests just how powerful an influence they can be.

"Truth is the first casualty of war."

An effective rumor has the ingredients of a compelling short story. It employs a simple, old-shoe, straight-from-the-shoulder plot, or a humorous or sexy plot. Usually it cites names, numbers, or places that are familiar and therefore credible. An authoritative source gives vitality to a rumor. The most virulent rumor rings true with roots deep in the cultural traditions of the area it covers, plus applicability to the current event that gives it rise. An effective rumor has a psychological bang which makes a person feel "in" as he whispers it to a friend.

Above all, the successful rumor has credibility. Then, as it gains acceptance as truth or possible truth, it spreads with an effect sometimes subtle and sometimes massive on public opinion.

A barnacle-encrusted story around the nation's capital has it that one senator exclaimed to another, "You know, they sound so logical I am beginning to believe my own rumors!" Thus men read into a rumor what they will. Men believe what they want to believe. And men, even deaf men, hear what they want to hear.

Rumors spring up like weeds, flourishing in such soil as wars and political campaigns, but they do not always just happen. They have been created, and sometimes mobilized en masse, by chancelleries, war departments, advertising agencies, and political campaign managers. They are "planted" at bars, cocktail parties, theaters, ball games, picnics, offices,

---

* Excerpted from Herbert M. Baus and William B. Ross, *Politics Battle Plan*, New York, N. Y.: The Macmillan Company, 1968.

subways, bistros, and boudoirs. They can be spread by professional rumor services, models disguised as society women, actors disguised as travelers, pretenders disguised as casual drinkers or event spectators—and above all when the conflagration breaks out of control, by amateurs. When innocent volunteers are infected, a whispering campaign can girdle the globe faster than a supersonic plane.

Let a man hiss a juicy one to ten listeners. Then let each of them repeat to ten others. At the rate of five minutes per narration, within less than half an hour a million persons will be in on it.

Coronet magazine's "Answer Man" said, "If you heard a bit of gossip and repeated it to two persons within fifteen minutes; if they each repeated it to two others within fifteen minutes—and so on and on—it would take only seven hours and forty-five minutes for everybody in the world to be informed."

Fortunately, rumor is nowhere near the effective and destructive tool it once was in political campaigns. As legitimate channels of communication have burgeoned across the nation—national wire services, televised news reporting, etc.—the planted rumor has subsided to the half-true, the humorous, and the innocuous. The vicious rumor is quickly exposed and often does its damage to the cause of its progenitor.

Rumor of the nonvicious variety can be the instrument of highest policy, deliberately wielded by those in highest places. As former California Governor Edmund G. Brown wrote in his open letter to Ronald Reagan:

Gossip, rumor and inside information are the nickels, dimes and dollars of life in government. It's not money that determines a man's place in the government sun; it's what he knows that nobody else does. And unless he spends a little of that inside information, who's to know he has it?

Then, too, most reporters would rather miss every news conference in a year than miss a single secret meeting. Finally, there is always someone at any meeting, secret or otherwise, who thinks you have it all wrong and believes the best way to straighten you out is to tell all to newsmen.

There's only one way to deal with this problem. Leak the story yourself. That way, at least, you are sure to get your version into print first.

Thus spake Edmund G. Brown on the clandestine netherworld of politics.

Democrat John Shaw was plowed under in the 1956 New Hampshire gubernatorial race in part because of a whispering campaign that he was a drunkard and secret drinker. The element of truth was that he was never seen to take a drink. He abstained totally from alcohol! But the rumor transfused church circles that he was a hopeless drunkard. "That's why he hides it. Why, he has bottles all over the house, but who could find them? A pity, what a nice sober citizen he *seems* to be."

What Do You Think?

1. Why do people believe rumors? Can people avoid being taken in by rumors? If so, how?
2. How do rumors get started?
3. What point would you say rumors play in shaping people's opinions?

8.   HOW IMPORTANT IS MONEY? *

How significant is money in a political campaign? This next reading offers some insights into this question. Does money shape public opinion?

Is $25 a vote expensive? Is $12 a vote expensive? Not so expensive as to wipe the grin off the physiognomy of the newly re-elected third-term governor of New York, Nelson A. Rockefeller, when he drank victory champagne the night of November 8, 1966.

Depending on whether one accepts the outside estimates of ten million dollars or the inside official figure filed by the Rockefeller campaign of 4.8 million dollars, Rockefeller's winning margin of 392,263 votes over Democratic Frank D. O'Connor in the 1966 New York gubernatorial campaign cost something between $25 plus to $12 plus per individual vote. The O'Connor people say they spent $600,000—and there was no visible evidence to make observers think they spent substantially more—so the Rockefeller victors apparently spent from eight times to sixteen times as much money as did the vanquished in that campaign.

Does this mean that money and the propaganda volume it purchases is the margin of victory in politics? Since 1904, the first year the two major parties began filing Presidential campaign expense reports, the bigger spender has won ten elections and lost six. However, four of those losses were to Franklin D. Roosevelt and no amount of money could have beaten him; one of those losses was by Barry Goldwater and no amount of money could have saved him. The other underspender to win

---

* Excerpted from Herbert M. Baus and William B. Ross, *Politics Battle Plan*, New York, N. Y.: The Macmillan Company, 1968.

was Harry Truman in 1948, and if Thomas Dewey hadn't overconfidently turned off the steam before the verdict was nailed down, he might well have won that one.

Political campaigning is a tossed salad of money and men. Money buys propaganda. The preponderance of money—meaning money when it is needed so it can be spent with skill, care, and intelligent planning— will usually be found on the winning side in politics because the contender with the heaviest and most professional propaganda barrage usually emerges the winner.

The 1966 New York gubernatorial campaign was a classic in evidence. Rockefeller went into that campaign written off as politically dead. He was as popular as measles. He was weighted down by the barnacles of eight years in office, an attrition which has pulled down so many others to political graves. As incumbents must, he angered more people than he had pleased with key decisions. Every time a governor appoints somebody, he delights one lucky winner and disappoints a number of frustrated might-have-beens. He was the open and admitted villain of two major tax increases, never a crowd pleaser in the political arena. Furors had been stirred over liquor scandals, the Empire State's version of medicare, and a few other [items]. Some of his closest friends assured him that defeat was inevitable. One polling expert said to his face, "You couldn't be elected dog catcher."

Then unfolded the most expensive campaign ever waged for a gubernatorial candidate in this nation of generously financed state campaigns.

Waves of the slickest subliminal TV commercials of our time were released starting as early as Independence Day, which is considered before the dawn in any ordinary November political election timetable. Estimates are that from three thousand to four thousand of these commercials hit the air waves before sunset on November 8—a deluge by any standard. In New York City this barrage cost, in round numbers, figures like $237,000 for one station (versus $41,000 for O'Connor); $231,000 for another station (versus $36,000 for O'Connor); $137,000 for another (versus $25,000 for O'Connor).

Also the state was inundated with more than 25 million pieces of printed matter, better than four for each New Yorker who turned out to vote.

The blitz included everything else that imagination could contrive and money could buy in propaganda, publicity, advertising, and printing.

A paid staff of more than three hundred people, almost two hundred of them garrisoned at headquarters in the New York Hilton, broke another record. While not all of these people were specialists at producing propaganda, most of them contributed to its effective distribution.

Printed literature is as useless as money in a mattress if it does nothing but gather dust in the headquarters storeroom. In this Rockefeller campaign a staff person was assigned to each kind of literature (there were dozens of different kinds) with the duty of making sure it got to the people it was custom-made to fit. If, for example, there was a meeting in any part of the state concerned with higher education, a paid worker would be there seeing to it that every one attending received a pamphlet presenting explicitly what Rockefeller had done for higher education.

Instead of the ordinary, easy, and economical campaign practice of just turning out a minimum handful of different publications, the Rockefeller campaign went to the very expensive trouble of designing original, colorful, hard-hitting literature, specifically aimed at every important group of voters in the Empire State—except those in jail, who couldn't vote anyway.

The National Observer quoted Dr. William J. Ronan, described as the architect of the Rockefeller campaign:

First, we wanted to reach the opinion makers, for we were afraid we had lost them. They just weren't articulate for us and I mean the legislators, the newspaper people, the leaders of various special groups. So we decided to approach them on a clientele basis. We prepared eye-catching stuff in each category—a brochure for the people in the field of mental retardation, another for labor, another for the fine arts.

William L. Pfeiffer, top organizer for the campaign, is quoted by the *Observer:* "It was out of this world. We had something for every group except the Times Square prostitutes." . . .

While there is plenty of evidence that money helps mightily to win political campaigns, there are qualifying conditions. The money must be available on time as well as in quantity for proper use, the incisiveness and class of propaganda materials weigh more heavily than mere volume, and if spending is too blatant and patently overdone it can end up doing more harm than good.

What Do You Think?

1.   How do you explain Nelson Rockefeller's victory in New York for re-election to the governorship? Do you feel he "bought" the election? Do you believe a limit should be placed on how much money can be spent on a political campaign? How would you enforce such a limitation?

2.   Sometimes the candidate who spends the most money doesn't win. How would you explain this?

9.   THE LOBBYISTS *

The Washington lobbyist works directly on Congressmen. He uses various kinds of persuasion to obtain what he wants for his clients. Here is an example of one lobbyist and his method. Does his opinion weigh more than that of the average citizen?

In a recent study of Washington folkways, Merriman Smith, veteran White House reporter, has this to say about the methods of a "typical" Washington lobbyist:

He arises when he feels like it, usually mid-morning, in a spacious, comfortable, but definitely unflashy home in the northwest residential section of town. Over breakfast, he reads four or five major morning newspapers. If interested, he skims through the Congressional Record for the day before. These are the golden hours of his day. He may earn his keep more from intelligent reading than from any other single activity. Years of experience have taught him to read between the lines and to search for indicative but seemingly small details . . .

Once "read" for the day, he may make it to town for luncheon with one or two key men in government at the Carlton or the Mayflower. Mostly, they talk about golf or fishing. Possibly in parting, he may ask casually, "you fellows heard anything new on depreciation allowances?" . . . This man is more effective for his employer than a dozen more energetic fellows patrolling the halls of the Senate and House office buildings . . . By being highly selective in his friendships, he manages to keep in touch with virtually any government move that might help or hinder his company. Our man's effectiveness would be destroyed if he had to play the lobbyist's conventional role in attempting to push or halt specific bills before Congress.

This description of the lobbyist at work makes him sound like a pretty casual fellow. A word here, a hint there, and he collects his fee. There is some truth to it, in the sense that the experienced lobbyist is a man with very sensitive antennae. And Smith correctly emphasizes the role of the lobbyist as a communicator. He is expected to keep abreast of governmental activities that may affect his client and to report these developments as quickly as possible. If legislation is in the wind that may hurt

---

* Excerpted from James Deakin, *The Lobbyists,* Washington, D. C.: Public Affairs Press, 1966.

his client, he wants to know about it early so that it can be nipped in the bud. If this is not possible, an early warning will at least give time to mount a counterattack.

So the lobbyist keeps a very close eye on the committees handling legislation that touches his client's interests. He cultivates the members of these committees and their staffs. He is an avid reader of the trade journals in his client's field. These publications concentrate on specialized areas, and when it comes to developments in these fields their Washington reporters frequently are ahead of the correspondents working for newspapers and general-interest magazines. The lobbyist thus has extra eyes and ears on which to rely.

The communicative function often is used as an excuse for not registering under the Lobbying Act. Some Washington representatives of corporations and trade associations do not register as lobbyists because, they insist, their only function is to inform their home offices on the status and prospects of legislation. A typical case is the Washington "rep" employed by a retail group with its main headquarters in New York. In describing his duties, he says that he spends almost all his time on Capitol Hill getting information from various Congressional committees. Asked whether he is registered as a lobbyist, he replies with a smile that he is not. Why not? "Because I don't make any attempt to influence legislation. I just gather information."

Lobbying, by the same token, is not quite as offhand or casual as Merriman Smith suggests. Most lobbyists work fairly hard and some work very hard. Their activities are not confined to palsy-walsy lunches with friends who have risen to key positions in government. They do get up to Capitol Hill frequently. They do try to push or block specific bills; that also is part of what they are paid for. Moreover, the working lobbyist is also involved in legislative drudgery—particularly hearings, the long, sweaty sessions at which laws are hammered out amid interminable talk. The picture of our man at work over martinis at lunch is incomplete.

Lobbying methods fall into three main categories: direct contact with members of Congress and Congressional staffs; indirect or grassroots campaigns to stimulate pressure on Congressmen from the public, and cross-lobbying. This last term refers to a common practice in which one special interest group gives its indorsement and assistance to another group on an issue in which the first organization may not be primarily interested, in return for a similar favor later. It can be summed up in the famous political maxim attributed to Simon Cameron, Lincoln's Secretary of War: "You scratch my back and I'll scratch yours."

Direct contact is the method most often associated with lobbying. Despite an ever-increasing emphasis on grassroots campaigns, the direct contact remains a prime technique. In his survey of 100 Washington lobbyists, Milbrath found that 65 listed the direct contact as the method they prefer and generally use. On a scale of 0 to 10, personal presentation of arguments to members of Congress was given a rating of 10 by 58 of the lobbyists. Only 19 lobbyists rated it below eight on the scale.

Approximately the same findings resulted from a questionnaire sent out by John F. Kennedy when he was chairman of a Senate government operations subcommittee. The questionnaire went to a representative group of registered lobbyists. Direct contact with members of Congress ranked first among the methods listed, with 43 responses. Testimony before Congressional committees was second, with 37. Printed matter—bulletins, newsletters, press releases and the like—was third, with 23. Contact with members of organizations, suggesting that they get in touch with their Congressmen, was fourth, with 16. The last two, however, can be considered grassroots lobbying; together they gave this method a total of 39 responses. . . .

However, Milbrath notes that some lobbyists feel that public relations campaigns are of use "even though they were not sure their message was getting through to the public, not to mention getting from the public back to the decision makers. They reasoned that the decision makers are quite likely to conclude that the campaign is very persuasive and [is] convincing many people how they should vote. Therefore, the decision maker may possibly alter his behavior in the desired way in anticipation of the reaction from his constituents, without receiving direct communication from many of them." Putting it another way, the massive public relations campaign, handsomely presented, oiled, perfumed and motivationally researched, intimidates the Congressman or bureaucrat before he knows whether anyone in the hinterlands is paying any attention to it. He reads the full-page ads and the facile brochures, is impressed by them and assumes that the voters will be similarly beguiled.

What Do You Think?

1. How would you define a successful lobbyist? Is the work of lobbyists democratic? Explain.
2. What kind of propaganda can lobbyists use to win public support? Cite some examples.

ACTIVITIES FOR INVOLVEMENT

1. These are two points of view trying to influence public opinion.

CUBA POLICY, From *Foreign Policy Briefs,* United States Department of State

CUBA, FREE-WORLD TRADE PERILS OAS AIMS

Secretary of State Rusk . . . declared that "those countries which for commercial reasons supply Cuba, especially with goods critical to the Cuban economy, are prejudicing the efforts of the countries of this hemisphere to reduce the threat from Cuba."

In an address delivered on the occasion of the 75th anniversary of Barnard College in New York City, the Secretary asserted that the continuing dedication of the Cuban regime to active terrorism and aggression in Latin America is a basic reason for the U. S. attitude toward free-world economic ties with Cuba. "We cannot accept the contention that trade with Cuba is comparable to ordinary trade with any Communist country," Mr. Rusk stressed.

The Secretary said that the Castro regime represents an "unacceptable intrusion" of Marxist-Leninism into the Western Hemisphere, and he recalled that two years ago the OAS declared it to be incompatible with the inter-American system. Noting that the OAS "has taken various steps to isolate Castro's Cuba and to curb its capacity to do harm," the Secretary pointed out that "it is considering further steps in order that the Cuban people may regain their freedom and rejoin the inter-American system."

From *British Record,* issued by British Information Services.

TRADE WITH CUBA

A British firm recently concluded a contract with the Government of Cuba for the sale of 450 buses. The . . . value of the contract was $11.8 million, including the interest charges on five year credit terms guaranteed by the Export Credit Guarantees Department. Cuba also has an option on a further 550 buses at a . . . value of $16.2 million, to be delivered in the period 1965–68. The order was secured in active competition with France, West Germany, Spain, Japan and Czechoslovakia. If a British firm had not secured the order it would certainly have gone to one of these other countries.

The British Government fully supports . . . restrictions, agreed to by all NATO countries, prohibiting the export of military supplies and strategic materials to Communist countries and it has faithfully applied these restrictions to British exports to Cuba. Nevertheless, Britain's very existence is dependent upon the continued success and expansion of its export trade. For this reason Britain must trade, in items other than those specifically restricted . . . or by other similar arrangements agreed with its Allies, with all countries, even those of whose regimes it does not approve.

In fact, Anglo-Cuban trade has declined appreciably over the past few years, . . . The Cubans are anxious to increase trade with the West generally. The British Government considers that it is better to encourage rather than rebuff moves in this direction, in the hope that it may help to reduce economic dependence on the Soviet bloc.

The extension of credit for the purchase of the buses was an essential part of obtaining the contract. The yardstick applied . . . was that of credit-worthiness. Cuba's balance of payments position is no worse than that of some other countries to whom credit is extended.

These are two different positions that tried to influence American public opinion. With which statement would you agree? Why?

Sample a random number of people in your community. Present half of your sample with the American position and the other half with the British position and ask them to express their opinions about American-Cuban policy. Find out if their opinions are influenced by policy statements. Then present each half with the opposing policy statement and again ask for their opinion. Is there any change of opinion? If there is a change, how would you account for it?

2.   One Congressman has introduced a bill into Congress that would protect the public from the "possibilities of abuse and manipulation" of political polls. The legislation would require pollsters to reveal their methods of operation, the composition of those polled, the period of time during which the poll was conducted, the questions asked, and the person who commissioned the poll. Would you endorse such a bill? Compare your feelings with those of your classmates. Then hold a class discussion on whether such laws regulating pollsters are necessary.

3.   Before the next student election, poll a random sample of students to find out which candidates they support. Compare your opinion survey with the final results. How close were your findings to the final result? How would you explain any differences?

4.   Using Reading 5 as a model, poll a random sample of your community on a current local issue of concern. Then poll your classmates. How would you explain any differences?

5.   Invite a poll taker to speak to the class about his organization and its aims and methods.

6.   Hold a debate or write a brief paper on the topic: "Resolved: That all political polls be abolished."

7.   Attempt to list the number of ways in which your behavior is influenced by the propaganda efforts of both public and private agencies.

Does the Government Have the Right to Lie?

Should the federal government tell all to the American people no matter what the consequences? Or should the United States manage the news so that public opinion is influenced in a positive way? These are two questions many thoughtful people are asking about information coming from Washington, D. C. Many are saying that the government is deliberately withholding information from the American people. From these concerns about the people's right to know has come the expression "credibility gap." This "credibility gap" is what this chapter is about.

1. THE GOVERNMENT HAS THE RIGHT TO LIE *

Does the federal government have the right to lie to the American people? Arthur Sylvester, former Assistant Secretary of Defense, feels that the federal government does have that right. Would you agree?

If I had been living in the early 19th century in what was then our country's West, and had been a religious man, I am sure I would have taken my stand with the Lying Baptists against the Truthful Baptists.

The issue that created the two sects arose at Long Run, Ky., in 1804, and posed the question whether a man with three children captured by marauding Indians was justified in lying to the savages to conceal the presence nearby of a fourth child. The Lying Baptists argued that under the circumstances he had the right, indeed the duty, to lie. But the Truthful Baptists shook their heads, uh-uh; Tell the truth and sacrifice the child.

The sects have long since disappeared. But during six years as Assistant Secretary of Defense for Public Affairs I often found the self-righteous descendants of the Truthful Baptists wandering in the same old moral fog.

As the Defense Department's spokesman I espoused the thesis that the indisputable requisite of a government-information program was that it be truthful. But I also stated that on occasions (such as the Cuban missile crisis) when the nation's security was at stake, the Government had the right, indeed the duty, to lie if necessary to mislead an enemy and protect the people it represented. For months the news industry, and others, distorted my remarks beyond recognition, howling that they were proof the Government was not to be believed under any circumstances. How hypocritical can you get? I know that it's axiomatic that fog hangs longest over the low places, but I can't bring myself to believe that fog alone accounts for the misinterpretation, misrepresentation and downright lying that tarnish the American news industry, written and electronic. I don't know a newsman who has served the Government as an Information Officer who hasn't been dismayed at the evidence of shabby performance by what he used to think of with pride as his profession.

If, as the news industry properly insists, the Federal Government has a complete obligation for truth, you would think the newsmen would abide by that rule for their own first principle. But they don't. As a wit has said, their motto is: "Don't get it right, get it written." Add to this a handout psychology, an incurable desire to prophesy and interpret, plus a failure to ask the right questions. Is there any surprise that much information about Government is misinformation? . . .

I was the Defense Department's spokesman during the Cuban missile crisis. President Kennedy was to make the fateful decision to force the Soviet Union to remove its missiles from Cuba, come what may. The overriding requirement was surprise.

During the momentous week of Oct. 15–22, 1962, President Kennedy interrupted a political tour in Chicago and returned to Washington. The reason given was that he had a cold. I didn't know whether the President had a cold or not, but on the basis of my 37 years' experience as a reporter and news executive, I doubted it. But because the explanation was simple and not easily refutable—who is going to say to the President of the United States, "No, you don't have a cold"?—it was as good as any and better than most of the cover stories I heard in Government. I shudder to think of the flimsy explanations held in reserve to cover some current and vital activities of our Government. But I could be wrong. For six years I watched cover stories go down smooth as cream when I had thought they would cause a frightful gargle. It was well that some, dealing with intelligence, did survive, but some others should have been exposed.

Certainly President Kennedy could not, and should not, have informed news representatives of the true reason he was returning to Washington: that for the first time the United States had proof positive—pictures, plenty of pictures—that contrary to their denials the Soviets had installed offensive missiles in Cuba, and that he was returning to Washington to consult with his advisors on how to counter the nuclear threat. President Kennedy was not dealing with some Indians about the life of a child, but with the lives of millions of his countrymen. If he thought the first step in fulfilling that obligation required him to contract a cold, he was joining the Lying Baptists, and so did I, and so be it.

On October 19, after consultation, I authorized a Defense Department release responding to questions about Cuba. The release read:

A Pentagon spokesman denied tonight that any alert has been ordered or that any emergency military measures have been set in motion against Communist-ruled Cuba. Further, the spokesman said, the Pentagon has no information indicating the presence of offensive weapons in Cuba.

A case can be made that the first sentence was technically correct. But the second sentence was untrue. The man who issued the release did not know that. I did. I knew that some of the Soviet missiles were operational. That meant that nearly the entire U. S. soon would be vulnerable to a sudden strike. I knew the President and the Executive Council had decided on a confrontation with Premier Khrushchev and were completing plans for it. I had been alerted that within 72 hours President Kennedy, in a report to the American people, would publicly demand that the Soviets withdraw the missiles and that he would announce the imposition of a blockade.

Newsmen, insisting they speak for the public, have argued that a response of "no comment" can avoid such untruths as our denial of knowledge that the Soviet missiles were in Cuba. But like all general statements, the assertion that Government information must always be truthful requires qualification, because these programs do not and should not operate in a vacuum. Government information may be addressed to the American people, to their adversaries, their friends, to the neutrals, or to any combination of them or to all of them at once. The newsmen's argument that the Government can easily say "no comment" is disingenuous because "no comment" is not a neutral term. Under the circumstances of the missile crisis, any good reporter would have been correct in interpreting "no comment" as a confirmation that we knew the Soviet missiles were in Cuba. An alternative would have been to take the inquirer aside and acquaint him with the facts on the understanding that nothing would be printed. Unfortunately that system works only sometimes. Without reflection on the inquirer's patriotism, it was decided not to risk the country's safety, in the name of the people's "right to know" and the Government's duty to "tell the truth." After all, newsmen are gabby.

It is really not the missile-crisis type of event that causes credibility problems. Nor does the refusal to discuss intelligence activities or new weapons systems, although holding the line on the latter is always difficult due to both industry and military pressures. It is the problems created in the Vietnam war by the absence of censorship and the presence of television that produce difficulties. I have often wondered whether critics think we should have called a press conference on certain tense Vietnam situations that have never before come to light. For example, early in 1964, with Vietnam already a very hot war, more than 600 Air Force F-105 fighter planes were temporarily grounded due to deficiencies in their propulsion system. My guess is that if questions had been raised we would have taken the gamble and leveled with newsmen and asked them to lay off. My experience is that in those circumstances the Pentagon reporters would have honored the request. But some itinerant newsman on the scene might have written the story, just as some itinerant newsmen damaged their country's interest by revealing U. S. Air Force combat planes were flying out of Thailand against North Vietnam at a time when the Thai government threatened to deny us the bases if any publicity developed. Newsmen in Saigon who had been briefed honored the request for silence, only to be beaten by the blabbermouths.

Government officials as individuals do not have the right to lie politically or to protect themselves, but they do always have the duty to protect their countrymen. Sometimes, even apart from military considerations, a program may be too tentative to reveal or there may be a question of timing the announcement. Sometimes, and those times are rare indeed, Government officials may be required to fulfill their duty by issuing a false statement to deceive a potential enemy, as in the Cuban missile crisis. I believe the Bay of Pigs was also such a time. But the fact is that this operation was carried on with such ballyhoo that the news media later accused the Government of Madison Avenue publicity tactics. So sensitive to the charge was the Kennedy Administration that it went to the other extreme in the missile crisis.

President Kennedy got to the heart of the matter when he told a meeting of publishers: "Every newspaperman now asks himself with respect to every story: 'Is it news?' All I suggest is that you add the question: 'Is it in the national interest' "? I would add only that when there is uncertainty whether the national interest is involved, the question to ask is: "Is this something that you, if you were on the enemy's side, would like to know?" I know from reading the Defense Department mail that most citizens—despite all the lamenting about the credibility gap and the Government's right to lie—upbraid the Department for releasing information they fear is helpful to our antagonists. They don't want their children surrendered to the savages merely so that the Government could boast it always told the truth, the whole truth, and nothing but the truth.

What Do You Think?

Should the government always tell the truth about its affairs? Under what conditions would it be all right for the government to lie? What about individuals?

2. CAN WE BELIEVE WASHINGTON? *

Otis Chandler, publisher of the Los Angeles Times, *comments further on the existence of a "credibility gap" between Washington and the rest of the nation. In the next reading, he distinguishes between international and domestic affairs. What insights does he offer?*

The title of these remarks employs a journalistic gimmick of which I do not particularly approve—that is, a question that really implies its own answer. Many of you have seen it in headlines. Examples:

VIETNAM PEACE MOVE?

DOLLAR TO BE DEVALUED?

and so on. Any story lacking a solid basis in fact can be, and often has been, written as a question. The net effect is to answer its own question; not authoritatively, not confirmed—but in the minds of careless readers, adequately.

I am going to answer my own question with what I am going to say. Obviously I cannot answer it with a simple yes or no. Neither journalism nor government is yet so computerized that, all the buttons being punched, a concise negative or affirmative comes bouncing out. . . .

[W]hat is truth to many is not truth to others. What is believable to some is inconceivable to others.

What historically matters is not the day-by-day record of apparent contradictions or obvious repudiations that flow from Washington today— what really matters is the ultimate achievement of the goals that this nation, through its constitutional elements, has set for itself.

---

* Excerpted from Otis Chandler, "Can We Believe Washington?" *Stanford Alumni Almanac,* April 1968.

Perhaps this approach may seem too pragmatic to some readers. It so happens that I share a strong devotion to the truth. But how many of us, believing a public figure's statement to be an outright lie, have subsequently learned that he, too, was misinformed, or not adequately informed, yet at the time believed his own statement to be the truth. Or that he felt compelled, by knowing the consequences of denying it, or the consequences of remaining silent, to believe it actually was the truth?

Howard K. Smith, a confirmed liberal and critic of government, in writing his farewell syndicated column, describes the "credibility gap" as one of the most distorted oversimplifications of our time. The President, he says, has to make judgment on facts that may be only partially known to him, "yet we tend to call it calculated deception if he does not instantly provide conclusive facts and admit failure. If he does not keep a frozen consistency, he is held to be lying. No government ever has been run that way and none ever will." . . .

"CREDIBILITY GAP"

The charge of a "credibility gap" between Washington and the nation is heard far less frequently in the realm of domestic affairs, yet it is in this realm, I think, that the charge has greater validity. Let us question, for example, the administration's sponsorship of legislation which it heralds as bringing a new era to the poor of Appalachia this year, and of Harlem or Chicago the next; when it talks of rebuilding American cities in a model pattern; when it boasts of fiscal economy in a time of monetary crises, while concurrently considering costly space flights to Mars and the maintenance of nuclear hardware to preserve the balance of terror in the world.

Should we not question the constant proposal of grandiose domestic projects when presented without adequate planning of how to operate and finance them, and without adequate safeguards against political squandering and bureaucratic waste? . . .

A THIRD PARTY

Much as we should value the reporting by the American press of foreign affairs, I think that what the media do in reporting our domestic developments will have a greater impact on our future. For it seems that the important role of the mass media will increasingly become what amounts to a sort of third party:

—A third party or intellectual force that always will be, and must be, a party of opposition . . .

—A party without the responsibility of directing or participating in government . . .

—But with the responsibility of criticizing and commending and independently investigating . . .

—Investigating both the party that is in power and the party that is out of power.

There are strong indications already that the media, both printed and electronic, are moving rapidly in the direction of this greater role both as independent critics of the party in power and as critics of the proposals of the party that is out of power. This has always tended to be true, for newspapermen traditionally have felt a compulsion to act as independent watchdogs for the public—to search out scoundrels and fools in government; those who cheat and steal; and also those who abuse their power for their own ideologies, or for the ideologies of those who elected them.

Representative government, in these nuclear times, cannot function if it becomes no more than the mirror of the follies of those who elect it. The abuse of power for political purposes is far more dangerous to this nation than cheats or thieves. The worst of all abuses of power is bad planning and fraudulent programming for political purposes. *That* is the kind of credibility gap that could destroy us.

What Do You Think?

1. When, according to the author, should the government lie?
2. Would you agree with the distinction the author draws between foreign and domestic affairs? Why or why not?

3. CLOSING THE GAP *

Here is a further position on the credibility gap which appears to differ considerably from the previous two readings. Would you endorse it?

Sooner or later, the American people will have to face the fact that the ever-growing authority of the executive branch of the federal government will have to be checked, if the democratic dialogue is to be preserved.

The President, leader of the vast executive sprawl, has taken unto himself powers so great that a serious threat is posed to the constitutional philosophy of checks and balances among the three branches of government—the legislative, executive, and judicial. Today, the checks and balances are out of order. Even though the First Amendment of the Con-

---

* Excerpted from Bruce Ladd, *Crisis in Credibility*, New York, N. Y.: The New American Library, 1968.

stitution set forth the principle that the widest possible dissemination of thought from diverse but equal sources is essential to the well-being of the people, there is doubt that our system of government is any longer dependent on the free flow of ideas in the marketplace of democracy. This doubt was anticipated by Judge Learned Hand, who said: "The First Amendment pre-supposes that right conclusions are more likely to be gathered out of a multitude of tongues, than through any kind of authoritative selection. To many this is, and always will be, folly; but we have staked upon it our all."

High among the President's powers is his control over the information which influences government decision-making and, ultimately, the course of our nation at home and abroad. The Constitution provides that the President "shall from time to time give to the Congress information on the state of the Union," but . . . the President enjoys wide discretion in fulfilling this informational role, and, in cases of unjustified withholding of information, neither the legislative nor the judicial branches has the means to force compliance. Further, the President's ability to command the attention of the news media maximizes his power to sway public opinion; yet, there is no guarantee that the President's influence on public opinion will satisfy more than his personal whim. In reporting to the people, the President is free to say what he likes and to omit what he dislikes. There is nothing to preclude his intermingling the "national interest" with concerns of a partisan or political nature. . . .

Walter Lippmann, a friend of Presidents for forty years, substantiates . . . the current credibility problem:

The credibility gap today is not the result of honest misunderstanding between the President and the press in this complicated world. It is the result of a deliberate policy of artificial manipulation to create a consensus for the President, to stifle debate about his aims and his policies, to thwart deep probing into what has already happened, what is actually happening, what is going to happen.

In its press relations the Administration does not hold with the fundamental American principle that true opinion arises from honest inquiry and open debate and that true opinion is necessary to free government. For [the] Administration, the right opinions are those which lead to consensus with the leader, and to create such true opinion it is legitimate to wipe out the distinction between patriotism and patrioteering and to act on the assumption that the end justifies the means.

James Reston, a proponent of the adversary relationship between the government and the press, also takes a dim view of current information practices in the executive branch. He says: "It is much easier . . . for the President to manipulate the Congress than to persuade it; easier to

overwhelm the press with statements, pronouncements, propaganda meetings, private interviews, messages to the Congress, trips to Asia—an
endless avalanche of activity which dominates the news—rather than to
convince the press that the President is following a clear line of policy,
and saying the same thing in private that he says in public." Reston
believes the President's technique of manipulation is applied at high cost;
the people want to understand and believe in the actions of their government, but they cannot. "Congress is told that it is the 'partner' of the
President in critical foreign policy decisions, but knows that it is not.
The press is invited everywhere, urged to report and criticize, but is given
the forms of participation without really participating and condemned for
the criticism it is invited to make."

Senator Mark O. Hatfield of Oregon is of the opinion that there is
an absolute necessity for the people to be sufficiently and honestly informed if they are to judge their own fates. "In order to function effectively
as citizens," Hatfield says, "the people must have access to the unfettered
truth. Without this access, our whole foundation of government will crum-
ble." Hatfield believes the American people must vigorously resist the
trend toward the government making available only information of a non-
controversial nature. "Of course there are certain qualifications to the right
of access, such as security matters, national defense, and international
crises, but the government has been relying on these qualifications too
often. The people are being asked to accept government on faith. Our
leaders have taken the position that an issue is far too complicated for
the people to understand even if full information is provided. The government restricts information and says 'have faith in us; we're doing what's
best for you.' This method is used on Members of Congress, as well as
on the public. It is an extremely dangerous practice." . . .

Can anything be done about the crisis in credibility? If so, who is
to do it?

In theory, the legislative branch—the Congress—is in a position to
exercise a great deal of control over the executive. But, in recent times,
the Congress has acted much like a dog at the foot of the master's table,
waiting for a bone to be tossed its way. The Congress has paid little heed
to its constitutional obligation to serve as a check and balance on the
executive. . . .

In 1966, the House-Senate Committee on the Organization of Congress received estimates that 90 per cent of all decisions in Congress are
made in secret committee meetings. A compilation by *Congressional
Quarterly* showed that congressional committees held 386 (45 per cent)
of their 861 meetings during the first months of 1967 behind closed
doors. When a member of the House Committee on Government Operations offered a resolution in 1967 to provide that a record of the com-

mittee's votes be made available to the public, committee members quickly rejected it. The same committee recently voted to limit drastically the authority of the General Accounting Office in securing information from the executive branch. The Congress also stubbornly refuses to allow radio and television coverage of its sessions.

If the Congress is to regain its station among the separate powers and begin to play a truly significant role in shaping effective, far-sighted solutions to the nation's problems, it must correct the appalling imbalance between the information it receives and the information available to the executive branch. In moving to correct this imbalance, the Congress faces a number of obstacles. They include:

1. *The fact that the preponderance of information about the day-to-day operations of the federal government is controlled by the executive branch.* While the Congress is responsible for authorizing and funding federal programs, it has no responsibility for administering them. The executive branch is the administrator. Thus, the Congress is dependent on the executive for information about government operations. It can be assumed that the executive branch will continue to resist attempts by the Congress to gain access to information in the executive's control.

2. *The decentralized organization of the Congress itself.* Authority in the Congress is widely dispersed among 535 individual members, two houses, thirty-six standing committees, and two political parties. As a result, it is extremely difficult for the Congress to bring its full weight to bear on the executive branch, The problem is compounded by the fact that congressional leaders, who are kept well informed by the executive branch, privately oppose efforts of their colleagues to secure information. These leaders understand that "information is power," and they are disinclined to share that power. Members of the minority party are not only unable to get assistance from the majority in acquiring information, but they are also stymied by some of their own leaders, who achieve personal security through "friendly relationships" with the executive branch and with the majority leadership in Congress.

3. *The fact that, in conflicts between the Congress and the President, the people tend to side with the President.* The late Senator Joseph McCarthy learned the hard way that the President had inordinate powers for rallying public opinion to his cause. More recently, Senator J. W. Fulbright has learned the same lesson. The President can readily command the attention of the news media; the Congress cannot. In addition to being at a distinct advantage in communicating with the people, the President also reaps benefits from the "age of Presidential government." In the eyes of millions, the President is above reproach.

In order to reduce the extent of its reliance on the executive branch for information, the Congress should develop its own information storage and retrieval system through the purchase of automatic data processing . . . equipment. The executive branch currently operates 2,500 electronic computers; the Congress installed its first computer in 1967. . . .

The Congress can further expand its independent sources of information by bolstering the authority of the General Accounting Office. The GAO was established in 1921 for the purpose of providing the independent examination and evaluation of executive branch programs. In 1963 and 1964, the GAO submitted 668 audit reports and other communications to the Congress on fiscal and related operations of the executive branch. However, after an executive branch official complained in 1966 that the GAO was "overzealous" in its investigations, the Congress voted to restrict the agency's authority. This unfortunate vote should be reconsidered and the GAO's responsibilities expanded.

Another major source of information for the Congress is the Legislative Reference Service (LRS) of the Library of Congress. In existence for more than fifty years, the LRS today is functioning under severe handicaps—insufficient personnel, outmoded resources, and cramped working facilities. . . .

The Congress can extract substantially more information from the executive branch if it will exercise cautious control over the appropriations process. . . . Without the funds provided annually by Congress, the executive branch would be helpless. The power of the purse is an ultimate power reserved for the exclusive use of the legislative branch, but it is rarely, if ever, used to force executive compliance with Congressional demands. This power ought to be employed as often as is necessary to convince the executive that "cooperation" is a two-way process.

Some changes in the committee organization in Congress would aid appreciably in overcoming the fragmentation of congressional authority and enable the Congress to be a more effective overseer of executive branch operations. One desirable change would be to place the Committees on Government Operations of the House and Senate in the hands of the political party other than the party of which the President is a member. Under minority control, the major congressional investigating committees would be considerably more diligent in seeking facts from the executive branch. Another proposed change, put forward by three members of the Joint Committee on the Organization of Congress, is for the House and Senate each to establish a new Committee on Procedures and Policies to monitor executive activities, with the committee chairmen being from the minority party. . . .

Another means for improving the congressional oversight function is to amend the rules in Congress to insure the minority party an adequate supply of committee staff positions. . . .

Finally, if the Congress is to compete on equal terms with the executive branch, it must abandon the cherished congressional belief that if something has been done a certain way for one hundred years it must be good.

The nation's news media can also contribute to the demise of the credibility problem if they will be more attentive to their independent watchdog role. A mere handful of newsmen regularly guards the press's right of access to government information; the majority do nothing. First, publishers and network officials can increase their now-modest investment in manpower in Washington, D. C., the world's biggest and most important news center. Washington news bureaus are understaffed and overworked to the point where only the most obvious news stories are being treated. Second, reporters can avoid involvement in the government's not-for-attribution and for-background-only press briefings. The service performed for the participants in these secrecy rites is far outweighed by the disservice they do the public. . . . "I think there are certain rules of hygiene in the relationship between a newspaper correspondent and high officials," Walter Lippmann noted a few years ago. "Newspapermen cannot be the cronies of great men. . . . I think there always has to be a certain distance between high public officials and newspapermen. I wouldn't say a wall or a fence, but an air space, and that's very important." Fourth, the press can be more alert to the news potential of the minority party. The minority has traditionally found it difficult to compete with the White House for news space. A minority with an improved communications line to the people would serve as a much more effective check upon the majority. Fifth, the news media can be less concerned with preserving the status quo and more concerned with raising hell.

The people, the first repository of the nation's strength, can do more than the Congress and the news media combined in assuring adequate and honest reporting from the executive branch. The American constitutional theory is that the people know best how to deal with their common problems. If well informed, the people can exercise their judgment and bring forth solutions far superior to those offered by any group of ordained leaders. As the 1960 report of the President's Commission on National Goals concluded: "Improvement of the democratic process requires a constantly better-informed public. . . . What America needs is not more voters, but more good voters, men and women who are informed, understanding, and reasonable. To produce such men and women in ever larger numbers should be a major goal of all labors to preserve American democracy." The people can vigorously and angrily express their disapproval when the government is caught in a lie or when the truth is withheld. They can keep abreast of public issues, make their views known to their representatives in the federal government, refuse to accept unacceptable answers, familiarize themselves with the records of candidates for public office, and—above all else—exercise the precious right to vote. To do less is to abdicate the responsibilities of citizenship.

In the last analysis, the solution for correcting the ills of democracy is more democracy. Those who say nothing can be done are clearly wrong.

What Do You Think?

1. How might Arthur Sylvester (Reading 1) reply to Senator Mark Hatfield of Oregon? Explain. How might Hatfield respond?
2. Would you agree that the news media should be "less concerned with preserving the status quo and more concerned with raising hell"? Why or why not? What does this mean?
3. Who would you say is responsible for the so-called "credibility gap"? Might many people be responsible? Why or why not?
4. Which of the many suggestions for "closing the gap" in this chapter seems to you the strongest? The weakest? Why?

4.   THE NEW AMERICAN MILITARISM *

Retired Marine General Shoup writes how the military establishment and defense industries influence major decisions of the federal government. Does the military have this much influence on the opinions of the American public? Has the military helped to increase or decrease the "credibility gap" in government?

America has become a militaristic and aggressive nation. Our massive and swift invasion of the Dominican Republic in 1965, concurrent with the rapid buildup of U. S. military power in Vietnam, constituted an impressive demonstration of America's readiness to execute military contingency plans and to seek military solutions to problems of political disorder and potential Communist threats in the areas of our interest.

This "military task force" type of diplomacy is in the tradition of our more primitive, pre-World War II "gunboat diplomacy," in which we landed small forces of Marines to protect American lives and property from the perils of native bandits and revolutionaries. In those days the U. S. Navy and its Marine landing forces were our chief means, short of war, for showing the flag, exercising American power, and protecting U. S. interests abroad. The Navy, enjoying the freedom of the seas, was a visible and effective representative of the nation's sovereign power. The Marines could be employed ashore "on such other duties as the

---

* Excerpted from General David M. Shoup, "The New American Militarism," *The Atlantic Monthly,* April 1969. Copyright © 1969, by The Atlantic Monthly Company, Boston, Mass. Reprinted with permission.

President might direct" without congressional approval or a declaration of war. The U. S. Army was not then used so freely because it was rarely ready for expeditionary service without some degree of mobilization, and its use overseas normally required a declaration of emergency or war. Now, however, we have numerous contingency plans involving large joint Air Force-Army-Navy-Marine task forces to defend U. S. interests and to safeguard our allies wherever and whenever we suspect Communist aggression. We maintain more than 1,517,000 Americans in uniform overseas in 119 countries. We have 8 treaties to help defend 48 nations if they ask us to—or if we choose to intervene in their affairs. We have an immense and expensive military establishment, fueled by a gigantic defense industry, and millions of proud, patriotic, and frequently bellicose and militaristic citizens. How did this militarist culture evolve? How did this militarism steer us into the tragic military and political morass of Vietnam?

Prior to World War II, American attitudes were typically isolationist, pacifist, and generally anti-military. The regular peacetime military establishment enjoyed small prestige and limited influence upon national affairs. The public knew little about the armed forces, and only a few thousand men were attracted to military service and careers. In 1940 there were but 428,000 officers and enlisted men in the Army and Navy. The scale of the war, and the world's power relationships which resulted, created the American military giant. Today the active armed forces contain over 3.4 million men and women, with an additional 1.6 million ready reserves and National Guardsmen.

America's vastly expanded world role after World War II hinged upon military power. The voice and views of the professional military people became increasingly prominent. During the post-war period, distinguished military leaders from the war years filled many top positions in government. Generals Marshall, Eisenhower, MacArthur, Taylor, Ridgeway, LeMay, and others were not only popular heroes but respected opinion-makers. It was a time of international readjustment; military minds offered the benefits of firm views and problem solving experience to the management of the nation's affairs. Military procedures—including the general staff system, briefings, estimates of the situation, and the organizational and operational techniques of the highly schooled, confident military professionals—spread throughout American culture.

World War II had been a long war. Millions of young American men had matured, been educated, and gained rank and stature during their years in uniform. In spite of themselves, many returned to civilian life as indoctrinated, combat-experienced military professionals. They were veterans, and for better or worse would never be the same again. America will never be the same either. We are now a nation of veterans. To the 14.9 million veterans of World War II, Korea added another 5.7 million five years later, and ever since, our large peacetime military establishment has been training and releasing draftees, enlistees, and short-term reservists by the hundreds of thousands each year. In 1968 the total living veterans of U. S. military service numbered over 23 million, or about 20 per cent of the adult population.

Today most middle-aged men, most business, government, civic, and professional leaders, have served some time in uniform. Whether they liked it or not, their military training and experience have affected them, for the creeds and attitudes of the armed forces are powerful medicine, and can become habit-forming. The military codes include all the virtues and beliefs used to motivate men of high principle: patriotism, duty and service to country, honor among fellowmen, courage in the face of danger, loyalty to organization and leaders, self-sacrifice for comrades, leadership, discipline, and physical fitness. For many veterans the military's efforts to train and indoctrinate them may well be the most impressive and influential experience they have ever had—especially so for the young and less educated. . . .

Closely related to the attitudes and influence of America's millions of veterans is the vast and powerful complex of the defense industries, which have been described in detail many times in the eight years since General Eisenhower first warned of the military-industrial power complex in his farewell address as President. The relationship between the defense industry and the military establishment is closer than many citizens realize. Together they form a powerful public opinion lobby. The several military service associations provide both a forum and a meeting ground for the military and its industries. The associations also provide each of the armed services with a means of fostering their respective roles, objectives, and propaganda. . . .

The military will disclaim any excess of power or influence on their part. They will point to their small numbers, low pay, and subordination to civilian masters as proof of their modest status and innocence. Nevertheless, the professional military, as a group, is probably one of the best organized and most influential of the various segments of the American scene. Three wars and six major contingencies since 1940 have forced the American people to become abnormally aware of the armed forces and their leaders. In turn the military services have produced an unending supply of distinguished, capable, articulate, and effective leaders. The sheer skill, energy, and dedication of America's military officers make them dominant in almost every government or civic organization they may inhabit, from the federal Cabinet to the local PTA.

*   *   *   *   *

The opinions contained herein are the private ones of the author and are not to be construed as official or reflecting the views of the Navy Department or the naval service at large.

1.   Should the American military make all military decisions without any check by civilians? Why or why not?

2.   It has been stated that the military influences decisions even at the local level of government. Can you find any evidence to support or refute this statement?

ACTIVITIES FOR INVOLVEMENT

1.   Write a short paper or conduct a panel discussion on one of the following questions:
   a. Should the United States government manage the news in the best interests of the American people?
   b. Do the American people have a right to be informed about all activities of their government at every level of operation?
   c. Does the President of the United States have the right to withhold information from the American public?

2.   Listed below is the Code of Ethics which newspaper editors use in publishing newspapers:

CODE OF ETHICS
or
Canons of Journalism
American Society
of Newspaper Editors

The primary function of newspapers is to communicate to the human race what its members do, feel, and think. Journalism, therefore, demands of its practitioners the widest range of intelligence, or knowledge, and of experience, as well as natural and trained powers of observation and reasoning. To its opportunities as a chronicle are indissolubly linked its obligations as teacher and interpreter.

To the end of finding some means of codifying sound practice and just aspirations of American journalism, these canons are set forth:

I.

Responsibility—The right of a newspaper to attract and hold readers is restricted by nothing but considerations of public welfare. The use a newspaper makes of the share of public attention it gains serves to determine its sense of responsibility, which it shares with every member of its staff. A journalist who uses his power for any selfish or otherwise unworthy purpose is faithless to a high trust.

II.

Freedom of the press—Freedom of the press is to be guarded as a vital right of mankind. It is the unquestionable right to discuss whatever is not explicitly forbidden by law, including the wisdom of any restrictive statute.

III.

Independence—Freedom from all obligations except that of fidelity to the public interest is vital.

1.   Promotion of any private interest contrary to the general welfare, for whatever reason, is not compatible with honest journalism. So-called news communications from private sources should not be published without public notice of their source or else substantiation of their claims to value as news, both in form and substance.

2.   Partisanship, in editorial comment which knowingly departs from the truth, does violence to the best spirit of American journalism; in the news columns it is subversive of a fundamental principle of the profession.

IV.

Sincerity, truthfulness, accuracy—Good faith with the reader is the foundation of all journalism worthy of the name.

1.   By every consideration of good faith a newspaper is constrained to be truthful. It is not to be excused for lack of thoroughness or accuracy within its control, or failure to obtain command of these essential qualities.

2.   Headlines should be fully warranted by the contents of the articles which they surmount.

V.

Impartiality—Sound practice makes clear distinction between news reports and expressions of opinion. News reports should be free from opinion or bias of any kind.

1.   This rule does not apply to so-called special articles unmistakably devoted to advocacy or characterized by a signature authorizing the writer's own conclusions and interpretation.

VI.

Fair play—A newspaper should not publish unofficial charges affecting reputation or moral character without opportunity given to the accused to be heard; right practice demands the giving of such opportunity in all cases of serious accusation outside judicial proceedings.

1.   A newspaper should not invade private rights or feeling without sure warrant of public right as distinguished from public curiosity.

2.   It is the privilege, as it is the duty, of a newspaper to make prompt and complete correction of its own serious mistakes of fact or opinion, whatever their origin.

Decency—A newspaper cannot escape conviction of insincerity if while professing high moral purpose it supplies incentives to base conduct, such as are to be found in details of crime and vice, publication of which is not demonstrably for the general good. Lacking authority to enforce its canons the journalism here represented can but express the hope that deliberate pandering to vicious instincts will encounter effective public disapproval of yield to the influence of a preponderant professional condemnation.

Try to summarize in your own words what the above Code of Ethics means, and then see whether your local newspaper follows these rules by reading it daily for a week. What evidence can you locate to indicate that the above Code is or is not followed? Compare your own local paper with

The New York Times or the *Los Angeles Times.* How do they compare with respect to following the Code?

3.   Invite a person from your local newspaper to speak to the class about the Code of Ethics for newspapers. Plan ahead of time by preparing questions like the following.

    a. Does the paper always adhere to the Code of Ethics? If not, why not?

    b. Does the Code of Ethics apply to all the departments of the paper?

    c. Does the paper have any additional or different standards to which it adheres?

7

Understanding Propaganda

One way to deal with propaganda is to read and listen to as many views as possible. In 1969 Vice President Spiro Agnew accused the communications media of exercising undue power over public opinion by their selection and interpretation of news events. *Is* this a problem? If so, what would you suggest to help solve it?

1. WHOSE FACTS DO YOU READ? *

How are our opinions formed? Can we rely on the mass media to present us with a "balanced" picture, or must we obtain such "balance" ourselves? Here is one person's view.

If a newspaperman has any special message for today's inquiring young people, he would say: Use the utmost care in ascertaining your facts. Remember that normal, honest individuals may differ, not only concerning the opinions and conclusions to be derived from today's facts, but concerning what are the facts themselves.

Don't accept only such facts as agree with your own preconceptions.

Suppose you were to note the facts—as regards Vietnam, China, hippies, the welfare state, the Pentagon—implicit in the articles in the *New Statesman* (London) or the *New Republic* (USA). Compare these with the facts on the same subjects as seen by *U. S. News & World Report* or *Time* magazine. You'd find a wide divergence. One needs to amend

---

* Excerpted from William H. Stringer, "Whose Facts Do You Read?" *The Christian Science Monitor,* December 26, 1967. Reprinted by permission. © 1967 The Christian Science Publishing Society. All rights reserved.

Marshall McLuhan to say, not that the medium is the message, but that the particular medium may, wittingly or unwittingly, color the message.

And what you accept as gospel truth will color your views and conduct.

For example, suppose you watched, last evening, a graphic TV documentary on Vietnam. It centered on the hardships and sufferings of the refugees, caused by bombings and uprootings. Suppose you supplemented this with an eye-witness story of refugee plight in your favorite news magazine or newspaper. I don't know about you, but after about three such encounters, I am ready to conclude: "This war is disastrous. Let's get out fast."

All right, but suppose instead you've watched a television documentary which zeroes in on American-Saigon victories, and some very worthy rehabilitation efforts among the rice paddies. And you've supplemented this with a dispatch detailing respected Ambassador Bunker's reasons why the war is going better, why constructive rebuilding is now possible. One may well come away from this experience with a belief that the struggle is worthwhile.

The point is, both sets of documentaries and dispatches could have been factual, accurate, from where the reporter, the cameraman, stood.

Recently a student came in to discuss a column. He had marched in a number of peace demonstrations. He told how TV cameramen had walked down the file of marchers, photographing only the long-haired, the hippie-dressed, the unkempt, avoiding the earnest, the neat, the middle-aged. This happens. The effort is not intentionally to deceive, but to catch the dramatic, the spectacular.

I recall two dispatches, appearing about the same time in the New York *Times* and a news magazine. Both concerned the over-all Vietnam picture. One reported the United States forces as thin-stretched, their strategies spoiled. The other said the American effort, at long last, was beginning to succeed. Which is one to believe?

Perhaps you are familiar with the well-known journalism class exercise. A simulated hold-up takes place; police burst into the classroom. Afterward, the students are asked to write their versions of what happened. Believe it or not, they differ markedly, and these students have been in training to become newsmen.

What's the answer? First of all, read a newspaper or news magazine that you feel you can trust. Next, read more widely. If the *New Republic* is your journal, read *U. S. News & World Report* as a countering force, or vice versa. Distinguish between journals of opinion and newspapers. When you're watching a television newscast, ask yourself if you're seeing the whole picture.

Cultivate a healthy skepticism. I said healthy. Not hate-filled. Compassionate. Discerning. Remember that most newsmen are trying hard to "get it straight." So are most editors. And if some have built-in biases, maybe you have too. Too often we seek out, take in, just what we want to believe.

Man has the gift of insight and intuition. "Seek and ye shall find." An accurately informed public opinion is a strong bulwark to any nation. You can help build that kind of opinion.

What Do You Think?

1. Do most of us "too often seek out and take in just what we want to believe"? Why might this be so? Is such a tendency good or bad? Explain.
2. Would you agree that "an accurately formed public opinion is a bulwark to any nation"? Why or why not?

2.   THE SCOPE AND LIMITATIONS OF PROPAGANDA *

Just how far does propaganda extend? Is it really important? What (if any) are its limits? In this last reading, we are presented with some conclusions as to both the extent and limitations of propaganda.

We have seen that the field covered by propaganda is vast, that it is an element entering into the most diverse and contrasting fields of human activity. The question we now have to ask is how important it is in these various fields. The answer will be fairly complex and we can from the start reject the simple and extremist views of those who say either that it is of no importance at all, a mere disreputable waste of time and energy, or (with Hitler) that it can move mountains and make black white or white black. . . .

[Propaganda] is at its most powerful when brought to bear on children and young people. This will be denied only by those who refuse to accept the word in connection with education. . . .

[T]he propaganda to which any child is exposed at school or in the home or church will certainly have a decisive effect for good or for evil upon his attitude and behavior throughout his adult years; though it may be, in the (exceptional) case of someone who for one reason or another does not fit into his environment, that his later life will display reaction against, rather than acceptance of, what was instilled into him during his early years.

---

* Excerpted from Lindley Fraser, *Propaganda*, Clarendon Press, Oxford, 1957. By permission Clarendon Press, Oxford.

Propaganda to adults is far more limited in scope. There are only two main circumstances in which a large scale propaganda campaign may be able to effect a decisive long-run change in [a person's] outlook on life and his behavior. One is if the subject matter of the campaign does not concern any very deep-rooted convictions or emotions. This case can best be illustrated from the commercial field. Far-reaching changes of habit have undoubtedly been brought about by persistent and expensive advertising campaigns . . .

This touches directly only the surface of life . . .

The other possibility of a long-run propaganda-induced change in people's behavior is in the field of religion. The word is here . . . used in the widest sense, so as to cover any creed or body of doctrine which not merely depends on faith as well as intellectual conviction but is also capable of exercising a decisive and permanent influence on the human spirit. From this point of view Communism, and even National Socialism rank as religious, even though the former explicitly and the latter implicitly, have presented themselves as irreligious and atheistic. From the propaganda point of view this is not a vital distinction: the essential point is the ability of the body of doctrine in question to inspire some kind of supra-national loyalty in its supporters. To achieve this requires, of course, propaganda. It is most easily achieved . . . among the young, who do not have to unlearn an old faith in order to learn the new one. But history is not without spectacular examples of triumphs of religious propaganda even among adults. . . .

But within this limit propaganda can and does play an important . . . part in affecting public attitudes and behavior. One French writer has described it as playing the part of a midwife in helping new ideas to see the light of day. Perhaps a better metaphor is to call it a burning glass which collects and focuses the diffused warmth of popular emotions, concentrating them upon a specific issue on which the warmth becomes heat and may reach the firing-point of revivals, risings, revolts, revolutions. If this view is correct, then we must certainly not deny propaganda its function in the processes of social change. . . . We have . . . propagandist literature such as *Uncle Tom's Cabin* [see Chapter 3] . . . It would be wrong and absurd to claim for the authoress that . . . she was responsible for the abolition of slavery in the United States. But no doubt her book focused American public opinion on the issue and so helped substantially to give the Federal Government the determined backing of public opinion in its fight against the Southern secessionists.

Several consequences follow from this view of the role of propaganda. The first is that in appropriate circumstances the politician will neglect propaganda at his peril. During the last thirty years and more democratic governments have more and more recognized the need for explaining to the public the reasons for measures they have felt it necessary to introduce. The usual method has been to set up "public relations" sections under a senior member of the various Government Departments concerned. . . .

And if it be rejoined that very often Government Department activities are not reasonable and are contrary to the public interest the answer is surely that if so that is not the fault of the Public Relations Officer but of his superiors. As the French writer just quoted observes, midwives have to do their job even if sometimes what they bring to birth proves to be a monstrosity. A burning glass is not to be blamed for the crimes of its user if the latter happens to be an incendiary. . . . This [is the] point of view . . . [of] Advertising (or Publicity) Managers. Their task, like that of the Government Public Relations Officer, is to explain to the public (or to the customer) what their firms are doing, convince him that what is being done is sensible and in his interest, overcome his instinctive mental resistance, bred of suspicion and conservatism, towards changing his behavior in the desired direction.

Secondly, and consequentially, the propagandist will be more effective the clearer is the message which he has to impart. This is an obvious principle in commercial propaganda, as in that undertaken at home for domestic Government and public agencies: any Public Relations Officer or Advertising Agent must know very precisely what it is that he has to sell or what the facilities of his product are which are to be stressed, what exactly his Government Department wants to persuade the public to do, and why. This same principle applies, at times less obviously but certainly no less strongly, in wartime political propaganda. Broadcasters to the outside world from a country at war, for instance, must know something of that country's war aims and of its plans for the post-war period. If they do not—if, for example, these aims and plans have not been formulated—then the propagandist will be well advised to keep away from discussions of these matters . . . thirdly . . . propaganda can be not merely underused, or misused, but also overused. This happens whenever the emotions on which it is brought to play are stronger than its initiators realized or can control. It is often said that revolutions devour their own children. What does this mean, if not that the original leaders of a revolution are too moderate to be willing or able to be carried along with the flood of emotions which their own incitements have unloosed? . . .

We come now to our last and most important subject, the relations between propaganda and truth. . . .

First, propaganda *as such* is neutral between truth and falsehood. . . . It is a technique or group of techniques directed towards a prescribed end, that of inducing a desired change in the target's attitude and behavior, and we cannot assert as an *a priori* principle that this end is bound to be achieved more effectively by true statements than by lies.

Any correlation between truthfulness and effectiveness in propaganda has to be established by appeal to experience; in other words the proposition that truth is the best propaganda, like the proposition that honesty is the best policy, is not *necessarily* true if by "best" is meant the best at yielding practical results.

Secondly, the "truth" which we are here considering is the truth of science or of fact—truth which can in principle be verified by the target. . . . The same consideration applies to the education of the young in fundamental questions of political and social philosophy. Totalitarians and democrats may each accuse the other of preaching false doctrine to the rising generation, but neither will deny that the other's propaganda may be highly effective.

Thirdly, propagandists may lie successfully even in matters of fact if they can be sure that their targets have no means of checking or verification. For that reason totalitarian propagandists are in general more influential in their own countries than are propagandists in countries where there is access to independent sources of information. Yet . . . in the present century, with the development of broadcasting from one country to another, the target may find means of discovering the true facts, or at least of realizing that what he is told in school or at party meetings is not necessarily infallible. . . .

Fourthly, propagandists can lie successfully even to targets who are adult and have access to other sources of information if *either* the propaganda appeals to a really urgent hope and will be accepted uncritically because of that hope—as in the case of the invalid or hypochondriac who buys a drug peddler's panacea [cure-all] . . . *or* the target has learned to trust the propagandist as having been truthful in the past and has no means of knowing that on this particular occasion he is lying. During the later stages of the Second World War Allied front line propaganda did what it could . . . to convince the soldiers on the other side that they would do better for themselves and their families, and could not hurt their countries' cause, by surrendering at once than by fighting on and losing their lives. This was effective propaganda. It was also as it happens truthful propaganda. But it might have been false without at once losing its impact. The Allied propagandists *might* have been laying a trap for their targets, cajoling the latter by promises which they had in fact no intention of carrying out (this was the story vigorously spread by the National Socialist and Fascist propaganda machines). The German and Italian soldiers who had already deserted, and whose voices were now to be heard over the Allied loudspeakers urging their former comrades to follow their example, *might* have been deliberate liars, the recipients of special favors by the Allied forces, or they *might* have been forced to act as they did by threats and terrorism. The immediate thing that mattered, however, was not whether what the Allies said was true but whether their targets believed it to be true. And many of them did believe it, being war-weary, homesick and defeatist, and to that extent defenceless against Allied propaganda (like the hypochondriac in the presence of a new drug); but partly, also, because Allied propaganda had in the past shown itself to be far more reliable than that of their own political leaders. Thus the immediate effectiveness of the Allied front-line propaganda efforts was due not to their truthfulness as such but to their reputation for truthfulness. . . .

Fifthly, however, a propagandist who having over the years built up a reputation for reliability, though he may lie at least once or twice and still be believed, yet does so at his peril. For his targets are not likely to forget it if they have been deceived on a major issue, one which for them may be a matter of life and death, and the propagandist (or his employers, those who tell him what he is to say) must not forget that his reputation for trustworthiness is an asset which if once thrown away will not easily be recovered.

Therefore (sixthly), the employer of propaganda, whether he be a military commander, a Foreign Secretary or the producer of a commodity for mass consumption, if he is considering whether or not to depart from the strict letter of truthfulness, must make a decision as between the relative importance of the short run and the long run. The more important long-term considerations are held to be, the more certain it is that "truth is the best propaganda." Hence the conclusion . . . that in the case of commercial propaganda, which in the modern world is largely concerned with a continuing impact on the target and is interested not merely in attracting his custom now but in retaining it for the future, truthfulness should be accepted, not merely by the moralist and the social philosopher, but also by propagandists themselves, in their own interests, as an essential ingredient of good advertising. Similar considerations apply to most forms of political propaganda. Do not lie in peace time if you wish to maintain your influence in international councils; do not lie in war time if you expect the war to be a long one; do not lie about your peace aims if you are concerned to secure that peace when it comes shall be secure and lasting; in short, do not lie if you are likely to be found out and remember that *in time* you are likely, perhaps even certain, to be found out.

It follows, seventhly, that lies can only be effective propaganda when *both* the target is defenceless—is in mortal fear, is hopeless, has no means of counter-checking the material given him or is unaware of what is happening (cf. the possibility of "subconscious sales") . . . —*and* the propagandist, or his employer, is concerned with the immediate impact of his propaganda and is prepared for its sake to sacrifice his future effectiveness. It is not to be denied that these conditions are sometimes realized. When they are, then honesty is not the best policy, however much we believe in it for its own sake. But the employer of propaganda must be sure, before he uses his weapon in this way, that he is not endangering or destroying its ability to be even more useful in the future.

Finally, it is worth underlining once again that the practising propagandist, as opposed to his employer, the Army or Big Business Chief, if he is to carry conviction with his targets, must himself believe that what he is saying is true; not necessarily the whole truth, because he cannot expect to know all details of military operations on hand, but at least not a gross distortion of the truth. The Goebbels ideal of a pure propagandist, somebody who puts across with skill and success whatever is fed to him without once asking whether it is true or not, is in terms of a strict definition of propaganda an imaginable concept. . . . The good propagandist may be cynical in detail (as the armchair student of propaganda must be to some extent if he is to understand his subject) but in the long run he will not convince others unless he is first and foremost convinced himself.

Thus the function of the propagandist is neither as important as some have held nor as disreputable as others have only too eagerly asserted. If conditions are appropriate his skill may be influential, in times of peace no less than in the conduct of war. But it will rarely be decisive—the field of education apart—and if it uses disreputable means it will before long destroy its own efficacy.

What Do You Think?

1. Would you agree that "truth is the best propaganda"? Why or why not?
2. Can a propagandist convince others if he is not convinced first himself? What does this mean?

ACTIVITIES FOR INVOLVEMENT

1. Analyze all the pieces of propaganda you can find in this book. What propaganda techniques are used? Which is most believable? Why? Compare your evaluation with that of your classmates, and then draw up a list of the characteristics you think essential for an effective work of propaganda.

2. Gather information on the propaganda techniques of a pressure group such as the National Rifle Association or the League of Women Voters. Form a committee to research the organization, and present a report to the class describing the group's objective, its activities, and its success or failure in achieving its goals. Try to obtain copies of their publications so that you might analyze them for their propaganda value. Then hold a class discussion as to how and why such organizations are effective.

3.   Compare the reports of an important current news event in two or three different magazines, newspapers, or journals. What differences do you notice? How would you explain these differences; what techniques are used by each to influence public opinion? Explain which article you believe is most objectively written and why. What conclusion can you draw from your study?

4.   Make a survey of public opinion. You must decide what particular questions you want opinions on, and the type of people you wish to sample. Here are some questions to discuss in making plans for this activity:

   a. What techniques would be appropriate—paper-and-pencil questionnaire, personal interview, or a combination of these techniques?
   b. How can you insure cooperation and honest answers from the people polled?
   c. How will you make sure that your sample is representative of the total population?
   d. How will you analyze the results?
   e. To what extent can you rely on your data?

5.   The following methods have been suggested as ways for dealing with propaganda:

   a. Listen carefully to many different views, by seeking out different speakers on a particular topic.
   b. Read periodicals with different points of views.
   c. Test any idea or product before buying it by seeing if it actually does what its advocate suggests.
   d. Avoid listening to individuals whose views are slanted.
   e. Determine ahead of time what your views are on a particular issue so that you will be able to recognize propaganda messages.

Rank these suggestions in the order in which you believe they would be most effective. Why do you rank them as you do? What suggestions would you add?

6.   It has been pointed out that propaganda may be used for good as well as for evil. Try to write a number of persuasive messages in which you encourage individuals to perform some noteworthy act. Compare your efforts with those of your classmates. Now reconsider the list you drew up in Activity 1; would you add to, or change, the list in any way?

7.   Interview a random sample of people in your community to determine how much influence they believe the local newspaper has in the community: Do they believe that the paper always prints the truth? If not, why not? Compare their responses with those of the class. What differences do you notice? How would you explain these differences?

8.   Invite a representative of the military to discuss the military-industrial complex and its effect upon American life and public opinion. Present him with a number of the statements made by General Shoup (Reading 4) and ask him to respond.

9.   Research your community to see if you can find out how many local industries have military contracts. Are these military contracts necessary to maintain the economy of the community?

10.   Write a brief report in which you attempt to explain how and why certain (e.g., religious, business, military organizations, etc.) interest groups in this country would be interested in influencing the minds of people in the United States.

BIBLIOGRAPHY
For Further Study

Books

ELLUL, JACQUES · *Propaganda: the Formation of Man's Attitudes* · New York, N. Y.: Alfred A. Knopf, 1965.

FELKNOR, BRUCE L. · *Dirty Politics* · New York, N. Y.: W. W. Norton & Co., 1966.

FREE, LLOYD A. and HADLEY CANTRIL · *The Political Beliefs of Americans: A Study of Public Opinion* · New Brunswick, N. J.: Rutgers Univ. Press, 1968.

GROSS, GERALD (ed.) · *The Responsibility of the Press* · New York, N. Y.: Fleet Publishing Corp., 1966.

HIEBERT, RAY ELDON (ed.) · *The Press in Washington* · New York, N. Y.: Dodd, Mead & Co., 1966.

KELLEY, STANLEY, JR. · *Professional Public Relations and Political Power* · Baltimore, Md.: Johns Hopkins, 1956.

KEY, V. O. JR. · *Public Opinion and American Democracy* · New York, Alfred A. Knopf, 1964.

LANDECKER, MANFRED · *The President and Public Opinion: Leadership in Foreign Affairs* · Washington, D. C., Public Affairs Press, 1969.

MOLLENHOFF, CLARK R. · *Despoilers of Democracy: The Real Story of What Washington Propagandists, Arrogant Bureaucrats, Mismanagers, Influence Peddlers, and Outright Corrupters Are Doing to Our Federal Government* · New York, N. Y.: Doubleday & Company, 1965.

MOTT, FRANK LUTHER · *American Journalism* · New York, N. Y.: Macmillan Company, 1958.

PERRY, JAMES M. · *The New Politics: The Expanding Technology of Political Manipulation* · New York, N. Y.: Clarkson N. Potter, Inc., 1968.

RIVERS, WILLIAM L. · *The Opinionmakers* · Boston, Mass.: Beacon Press, 1965.

ROURKE, FRANCIS · *Secrecy Versus Publicity* · Baltimore, Md.: Johns Hopkins, 1960.

SMITH, RALPH LEE · *The Bargain Hucksters* · Binghamton, New York, N. Y.: Vail-Ballou Press, 1962.

TAPLIN, WALTER · *Advertising: A New Approach* · Boston, Mass.: Little, Brown & Co., 1963.

THAYER, GEORGE · *The Farther Shores of Politics: The American Political Fringe Today* · New York, N. Y.: Simon and Schuster, 1967.

TYLER, POYNTZ · *Advertising in America* · New York, N. Y.: H. W. Wilson, 1959.

WHITAKER, URBAN G., JR. (ed.) · *Propaganda and International Relations* · San Francisco, Cal.: Howard Chandler, 1960.

Games

ALLEN, ROBERT W. and LORNE GREENS · *The Propaganda Game* · Fort Lauderdale, Florida, Nova Academic Games Project, Nova High School, 1966.

Credibility Gap: A Contemporary Citizens' Game · Waltham, Mass., American Publishing Corp., 1967.

Paperback Books

BANFIELD, EDWARD C. · *Political Influence* · Garden City, N. Y.: Doubleday Anchor Books.

BARBU, ZEVEDAI · *Democracy & Dictatorship* · New York, N. Y.: Grove Press.

BUCKLEY, WILLIAM F. JR. · *Rumbles Left & Right* · New York, N. Y.: Macfadden.

CATER, DOUGLASS · *Fourth Branch of Government* · New York, N. Y.: Vintage Books.

CLARK, KENNETH B. · *Dark Ghetto: Dilemmas of Social Power* · New York, N. Y.: Torchbooks.

DOMHOFF, G. W. · *Who Rules America* · Englewood Cliffs, N. J.: Spectrum Books.

FROMM, ERICH · *Escape from Freedom* · New York, N. Y.: An Avon Library Book.

GLIM, AESOP · *How Advertising Is Written and Why* · New York, N. Y.: Dover.

GOLDING, WILLIAM · *Lord of the Flies* · New York, N. Y.: Capricorn Books.

HALL, EDWARD T. · *Silent Language* · New York, N. Y.: Premier Books.

HOFFER, ERIC · *True Believer* · New York, N. Y.: Perennial Library.

HOOVER, J. EDGAR · *Masters of Deceit* · New York, N. Y.: Pocket Books.

LIPPMANN, WALTER · *Public Opinion* · New York, N. Y.: Free Press.

MASTERS, DEXTER · *The Intelligent Buyers' Guide to Sellers* · Mount Vernon, N. Y.: Consumers' Union.

MITCHELL, MALCOLM G. and ROBERT F. MADGIC · *Nominating Conventions and the Electoral College* · Englewood Cliffs, N. J.: Scholastic Book Services.

OVERSTREET, HARRY and BONARO · *What We Must Know About Communism* · New York, N. Y.: Pocket Books.
PACKARD, VANCE · *Hidden Persuaders* · New York, N. Y.: Pocket Books.
———— · *Status Seekers* · New York, N. Y.: Pocket Books.
———— · *Waste Makers* · New York, N. Y.: Pocket Books.
REMMERS, H. H. and D. H. RADLER · *The American Teenager* · New York, N. Y.: Charter Books.
REISMAN, DAVID *et al* · *The Lonely Crowd: A Study of the Changing American Character* · Garden City, N. Y.: Doubleday Anchor Books.
SORENSEN, THEODORE C. · *Decision-Making in the White House* · New York, N. Y.: Columbia Univ. Press.
WARBURG, JAMES P. · *Reveille for Rebels: A Book for Americans of Pre-voting Age* · Garden City, N. Y.: Doubleday & Co.
WHYTE, WILLIAM H. JR. · *Organization Man* · Garden City, N. Y.: Doubleday Anchor Books.

Booklets

OLIVER, DONALD W. and FRED M. NEWMANN · *Community Change: Law, Politics, and Social Attitudes* · Middletown, Conn.: American Education Publications.
———— · *Municipal Politics: Interest Groups and the Government* · Middletown, Conn.: American Education Publications.
STANTON, GORDON and NOEL H. LEIGH-TAYLOR · *I Protest: Dissent and Decision—The Democratic Way* · Stamford, Conn.: Youth Education Systems.

Articles

BURNHAM, JAMES · "Their NLF's and Ours," *National Review,* April 8, 1969.
COMMAGER, HENRY STEELE · "On the Way to 1984," *Saturday Review,* April 15, 1967.
DAVISON, W. P. · "Political Communication As an Instrument of Foreign Policy," *Public Opinion Quarterly,* Spring, 1963.
HORN, JOHN · "Television," *The Nation,* March 11, 1968. (See letter of reply "Command Performance" by Lawrence E. Spivak, *The Nation,* April 8, 1968.)
"Ideas in Action: Revolutionary Gurus," *Newsweek,* May 6, 1968.
"Now U. S. Has One Propaganda Voice in Vietnam," *U. S. News and World Report,* April 19, 1965.
"Politics of Patronage," *Senior Scholastic,* May 9, 1969.
SCHWARZ, H. G. · "America Faces Asia: The Problem of Image Projection," *Journal of Politics,* August, 1964.
TAYLOR, E. · "Political Warfare," *The Reporter,* September 14, 1961.

"The War We're Losing: Communications Crisis: What Can Persuaders Do? " *Printers' Ink,* September 14, 1963.

Films, Filmstrips, Recordings

Brainwashing (60 min; B/W; Association Films) · A documentary film in which victims of "brainwashing" discuss and illustrate Communist psychological techniques used to induce them to reveal sought information.

Characteristics of the Electorate (20 min; B/W; Modern Learning Aids) · A description of how people vote and an analysis of the key groups that make up our population. Dr. Claude Robinson, chairman of the Board, Opinion Research Corp., analyzes the political composition of our population and the behavior of the American electorate.

Communist Accent on Youth (30 min; B/W; prod. Pepperdine College) · Explores how basic philosophies of Communism contrast with those of a free country; how Communist leaders think and act and how they manipulate and exploit students and youth throughout the world to serve their avowed goal of world Communism.

Dictatorship: Hitler, A Case Study (prod. Popular Science Publishing Co.) · By examining the career of Adolf Hitler in Germany, this filmstrip studies the conditions which lead to dictatorship, the techniques which enable dictators to maintain power, and the consequences of this form of government.

Conformity (40 min; B/W; Sterling Films) · Harry Reasoner narrates this probe into the controversial subject of conformity and the corresponding right of dissent. Several real-life situations are posed, showing the benefits of free dissent and the harm of rigid conformity.

"I Have A Dream . . .": The Life of Martin Luther King, Jr. (35 min; B/W; prod. C.B.S. News) · The story of this dedicated man's life, and the forces that brought him to the leadership of his people are explored, with actual news film footage. The film brings a better understanding of the philosophies and ideals that he exemplified. In telling the story of Dr. King, the civil rights movement of the 1950's and 60's plays an integral part.

Man of Conscience (28 min; B/W; prod. CBS News) · Meet A. J. Muste, Christian minister, teacher, labor leader, civil rights leader, but first and foremost a pacifist. Because of his beliefs, he lost his first full-time ministry. Muste's subsequent ministries became centers of pacifist activity as he became active in many pacifist organizations and movements.

Not for Conquest (28 min; color, prod. U. S. Dept. of Defense) · A propaganda film on the combat readiness of the Armed Forces along with a review of the actions over the past five years which have brought forth the present concept of flexibility. Highlights such diverse actions as Vietnam, the Dominican Republic, earthquake relief in Central America, and civic action.

Persuasion Techniques and Propaganda (prod. Popular Science Publishing Co.) · Filmstrip analyzing the role of public opinion in economic and public affairs, the techniques by which public opinion is formed and how it is expressed. Explains and illustrates the methods by which propaganda and persuasion techniques can be detected, e.g., identification devices, glittering generalities, and big lies.

Point of Order (97 min; B/W; Continental 16, Inc.) · A documentary film composed of the most dramatic and memorable events of the Army-McCarthy hearings of 1954. The sequences were taken from television films shot during the actual hearings.

Pollsters and Politics (26 min; B/W; Association Instructional Materials) · How polls are taken and how they are used as a tool of political campaigns. This is part of the CBS Television Network, Twentieth Century series.

Pressure Groups in Action (20 min; B/W; Modern Learning Aids) · The importance of pressure groups and the need for them in our democratic political system. Dr. Marbury Ogle, professor of government, Purdue Univ., explains the techniques used by such groups and their effects.

"Sinews of Peace" Address (33⅓ r.p.m. L.P., Spoken Arts) · The historic speech delivered by the late Sir Winston Churchill, former prime minister of England, at Westminster College, Fulton, Missouri, on March 5, 1946.

Smear: The Game of Dirty Politics (26 min; B/W; Association Instructional Materials) · Takes a look at the techniques of the "big lie" and some of the famous smears of past Presidential-election campaigns. One of the CBS Television Network, Twentieth Century series.

Star-Spangled Extremists (28 min; B/W; prod. Anti-Defamation League) · Examines the tactics of right-wing extremists as they launch attacks on schools, libraries, and PTA groups, and question the loyalty of political leaders. Professor Alan Westin of Columbia Univ. points up the characteristics of the radical right wing.

Waging a Campaign and Winning an Election (20 min; B/W; Modern Learning Aids) · Portrays the problems involved in electing a candidate to office. Mr. Robert Humphreys, former campaign director for the Republican National Committee, shows how campaign strategy is developed in an exciting and practical way.

Who Shapes U. S. Policy? (70 frs; prod. *The New York Times*) · Looks at the democratic process of decision-making. Shows the roles played by the President, the State Department, members of the Senate Foreign Relations Committee, pressure groups, and others in making major foreign policy decisions. Recent case histories illustrate this process in action.